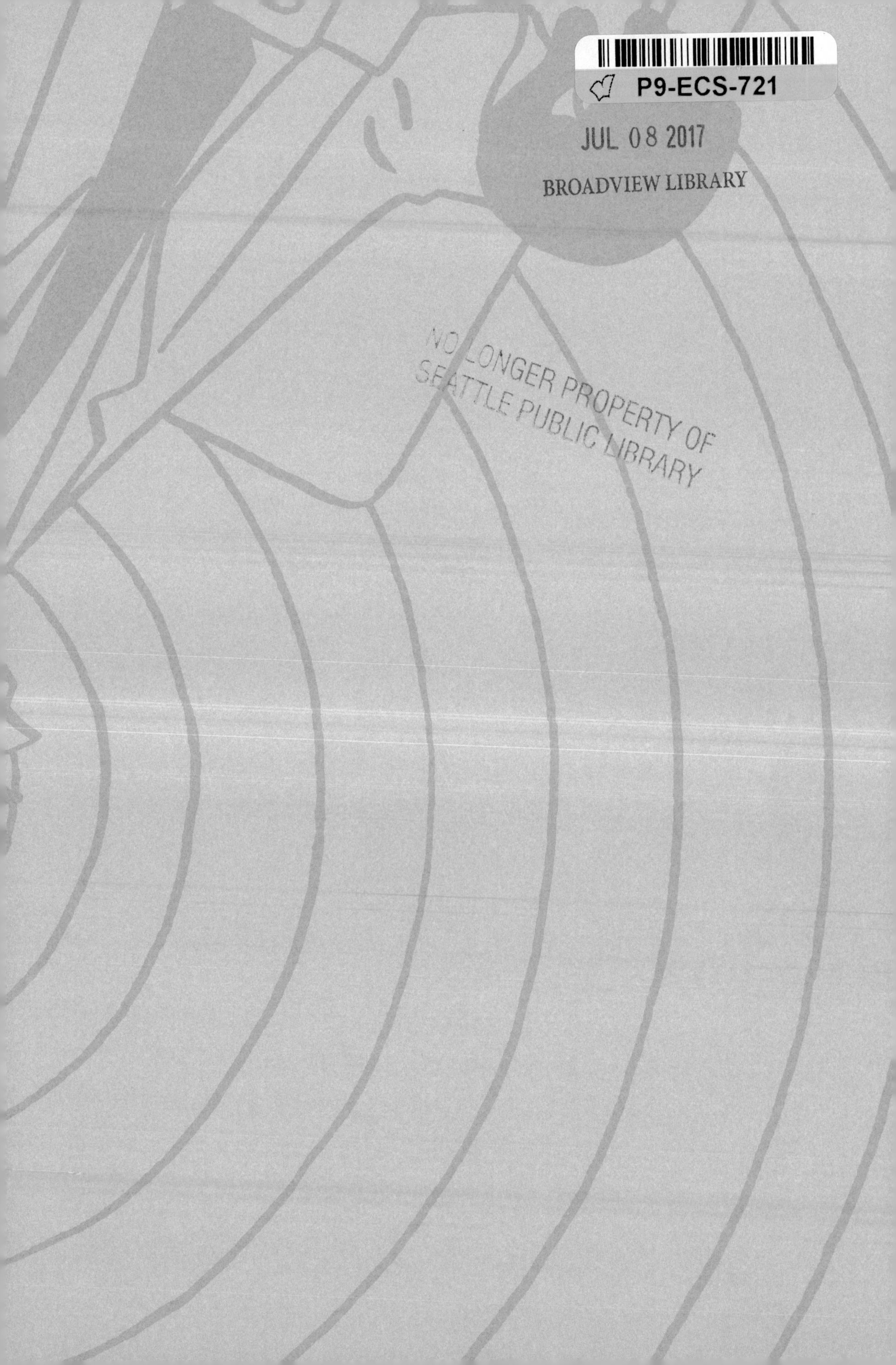

I KILLED
ADOLF
HITLER

I Killed Adolf Hitler
Tenth Anniversary Edition

FANTAGRAPHICS BOOKS
7563 Lake City Way NE
Seattle, WA 98115

www.fantagraphics.com

Designed by Jason and Covey
Lettered by Paul Baresh
Edited and translated by Kim Thompson
Associate Publisher: Eric Reynolds
Publisher: Gary Groth

First printing: May 2017
ISBN: 978-1-68396-008-9

Printed in China

I KILLED ADOLF HITLER

by JASON

Colored by HUBERT

FANTAGRAPHICS BOOKS

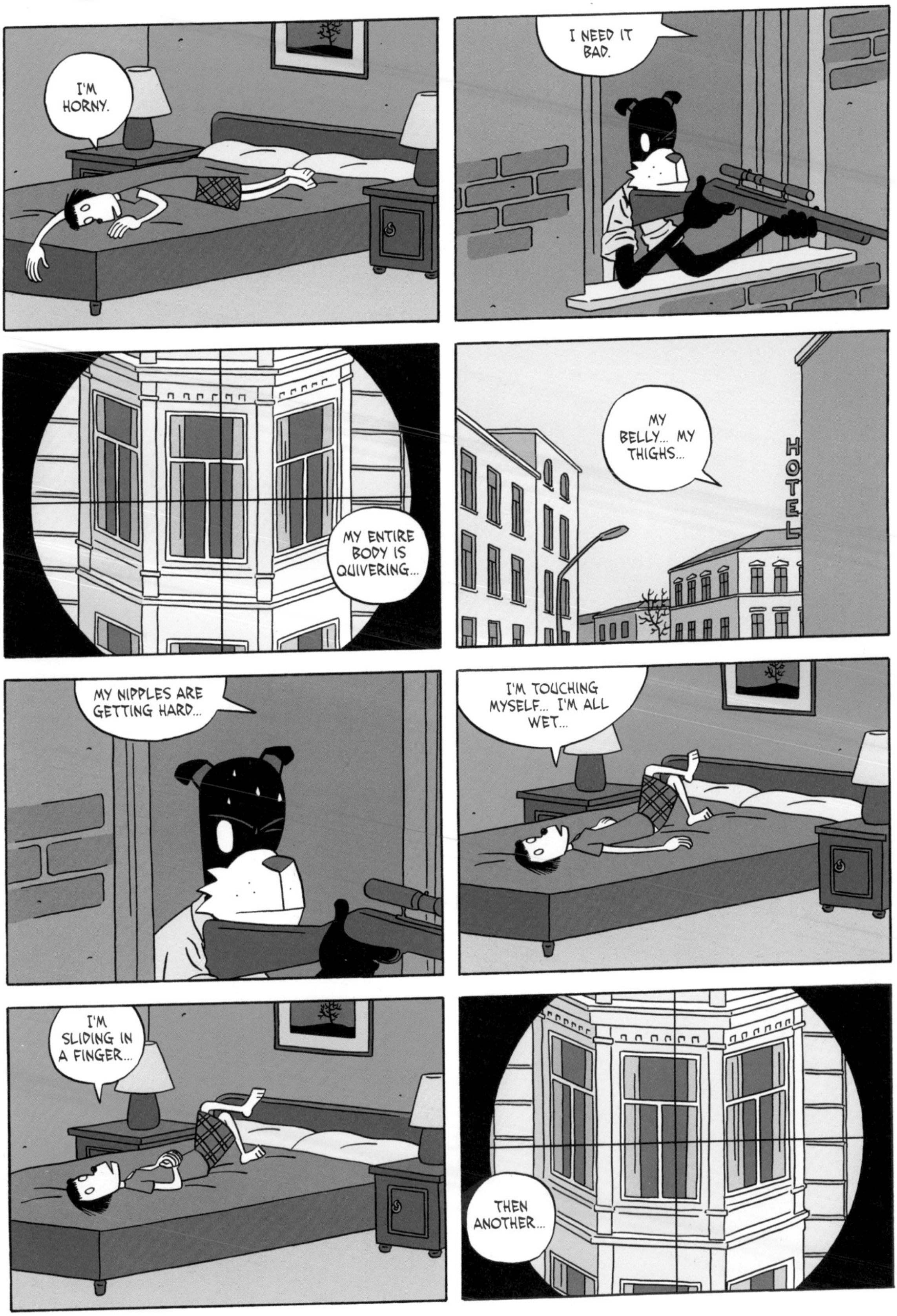
I'M HORNY.
I NEED IT BAD.
MY ENTIRE BODY IS QUIVERING...
MY BELLY... MY THIGHS...
HOTEL
MY NIPPLES ARE GETTING HARD...
I'M TOUCHING MYSELF... I'M ALL WET...
I'M SLIDING IN A FINGER...
THEN ANOTHER...

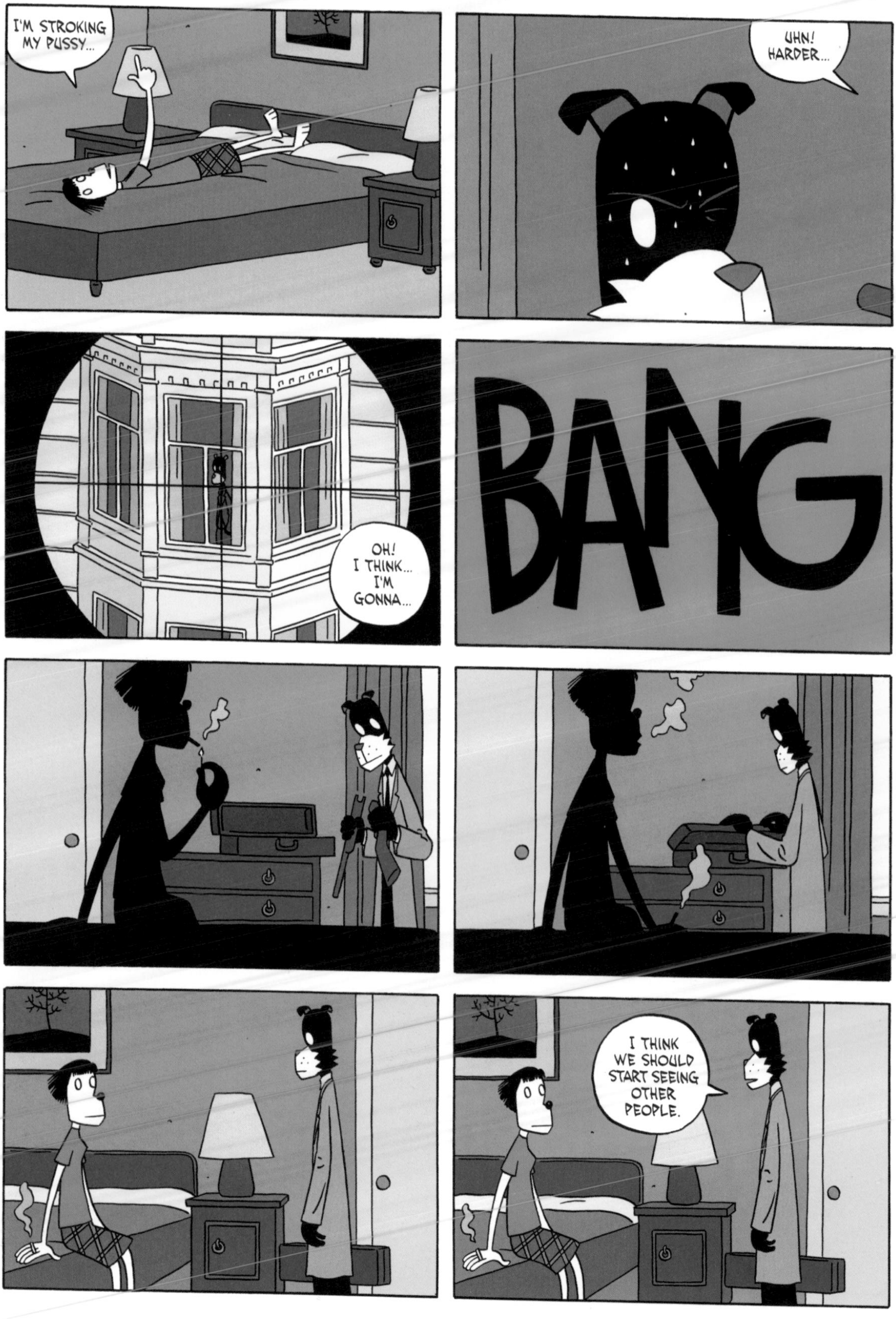
I'M STROKING MY PUSSY...
UHN! HARDER...
OH! I THINK... I'M GONNA...
BANG
I THINK WE SHOULD START SEEING OTHER PEOPLE.

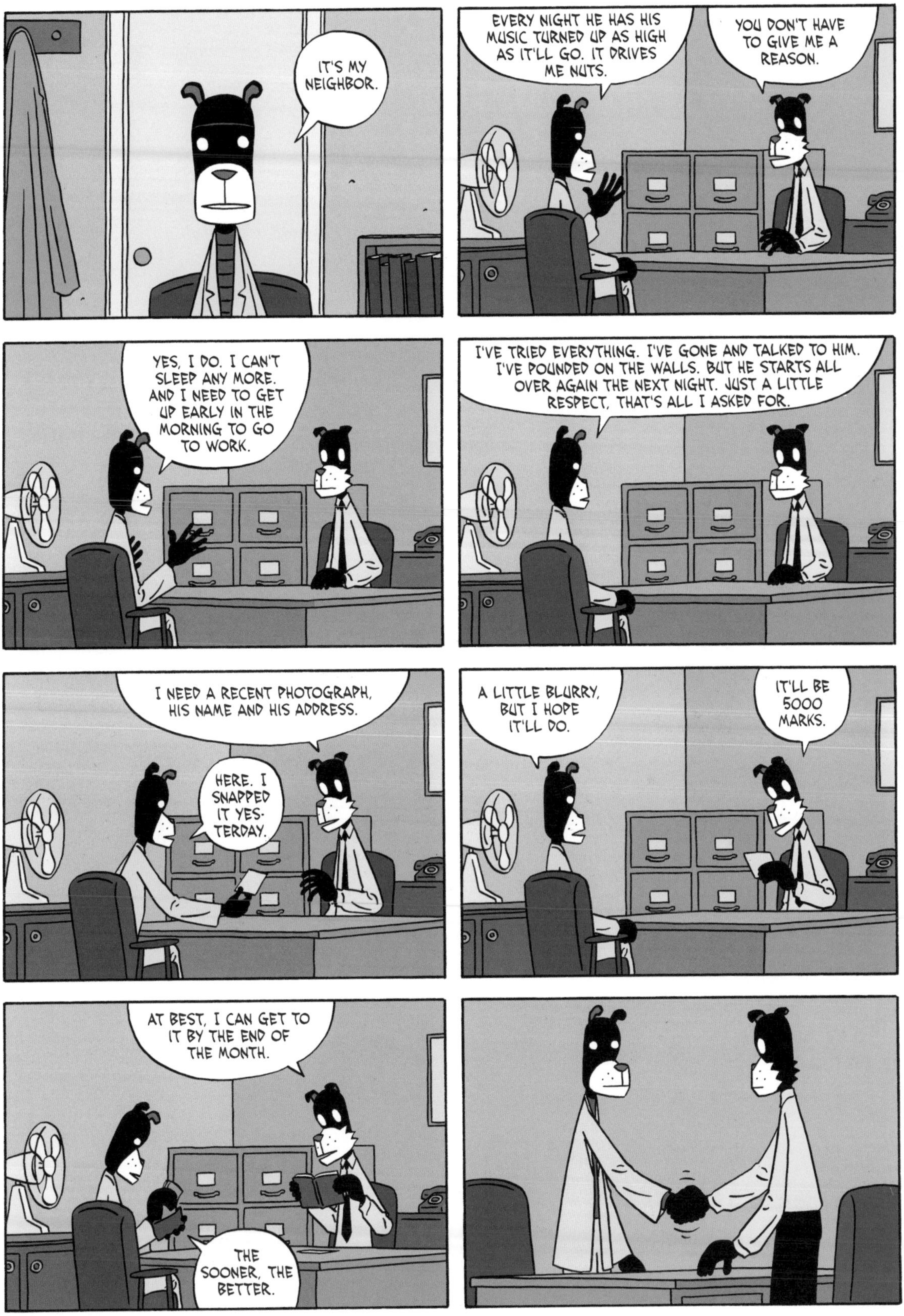
IT'S MY NEIGHBOR.
EVERY NIGHT HE HAS HIS MUSIC TURNED UP AS HIGH AS IT'LL GO. IT DRIVES ME NUTS.
YOU DON'T HAVE TO GIVE ME A REASON.
YES, I DO. I CAN'T SLEEP ANY MORE. AND I NEED TO GET UP EARLY IN THE MORNING TO GO TO WORK.
I'VE TRIED EVERYTHING. I'VE GONE AND TALKED TO HIM. I'VE POUNDED ON THE WALLS. BUT HE STARTS ALL OVER AGAIN THE NEXT NIGHT. JUST A LITTLE RESPECT, THAT'S ALL I ASKED FOR.
I NEED A RECENT PHOTOGRAPH, HIS NAME AND HIS ADDRESS.
HERE. I SNAPPED IT YES-TERDAY.
A LITTLE BLURRY, BUT I HOPE IT'LL DO.
IT'LL BE 5000 MARKS.
AT BEST, I CAN GET TO IT BY THE END OF THE MONTH.
THE SOONER, THE BETTER.

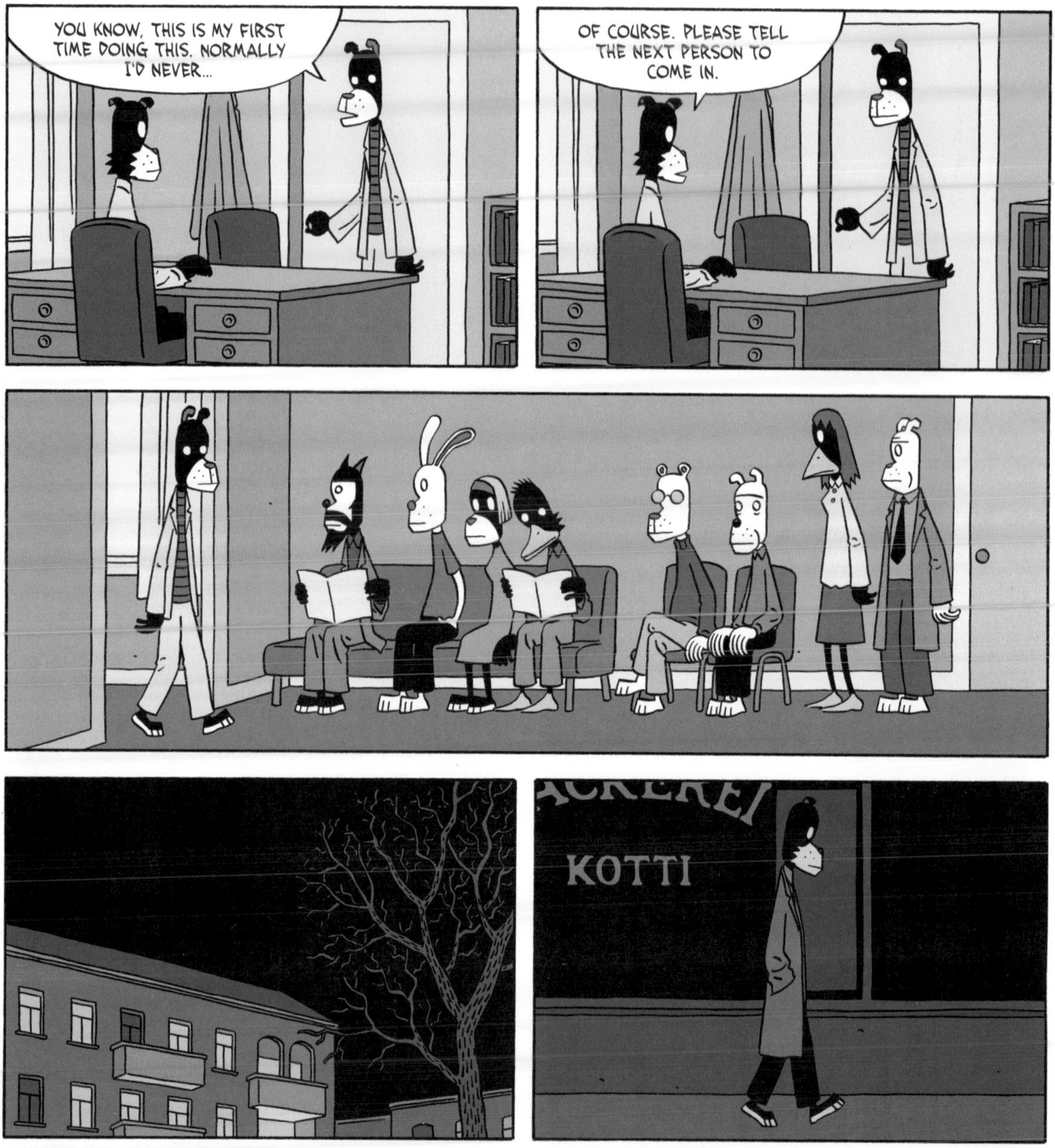
YOU KNOW, THIS IS MY FIRST TIME DOING THIS. NORMALLY I'D NEVER...
OF COURSE. PLEASE TELL THE NEXT PERSON TO COME IN.
KOTTI
BANG!

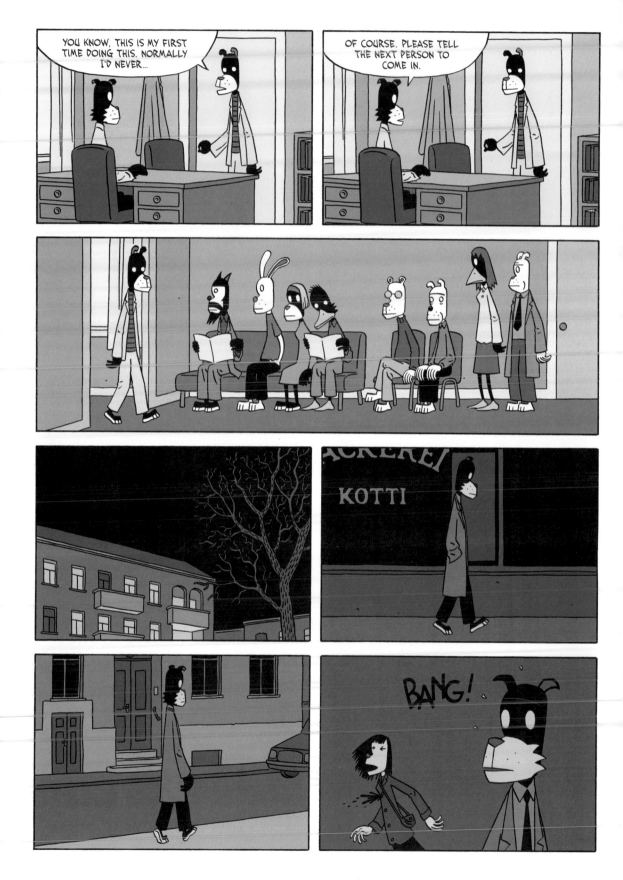

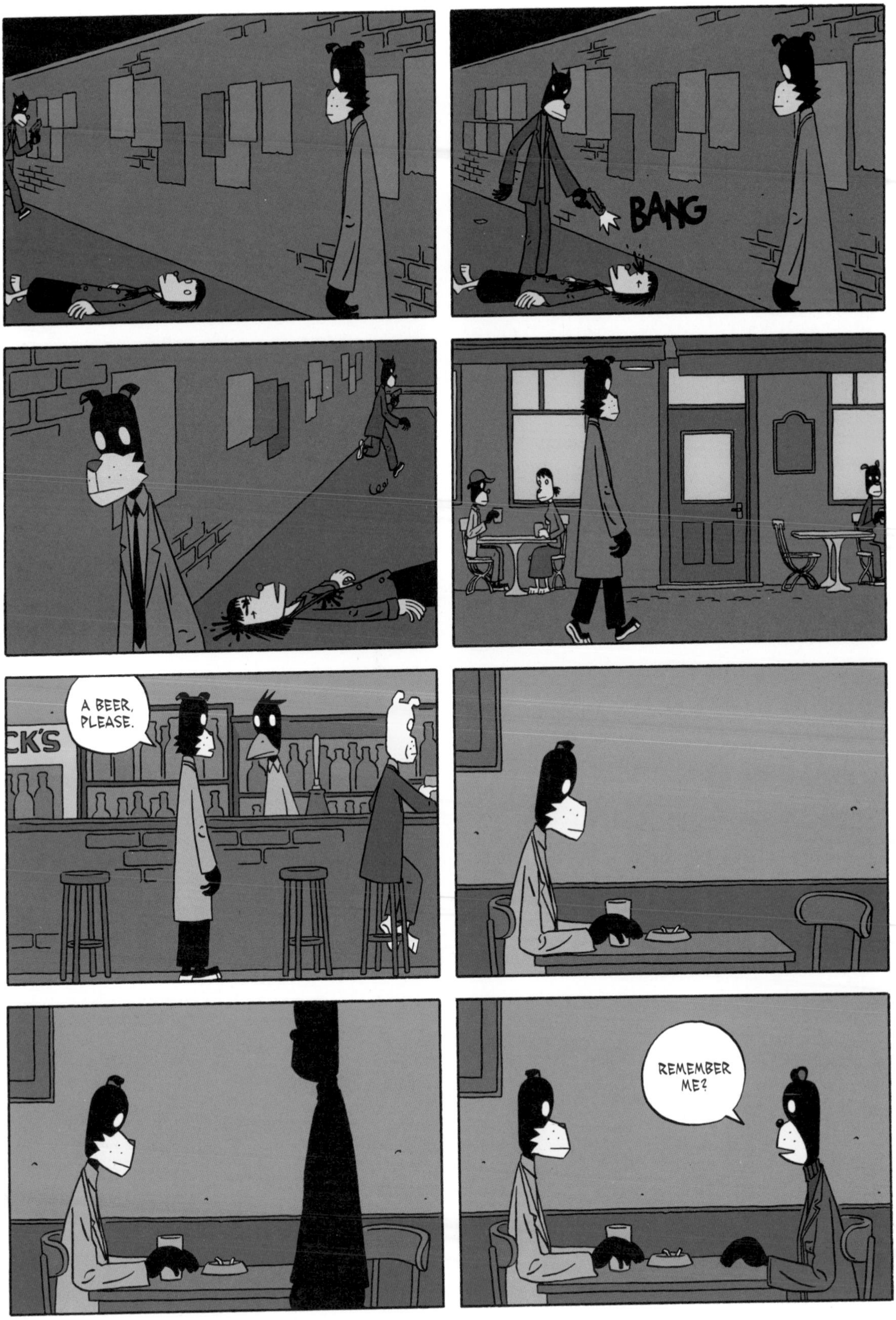
BANG
A BEER, PLEASE.
CK'S
REMEMBER ME?

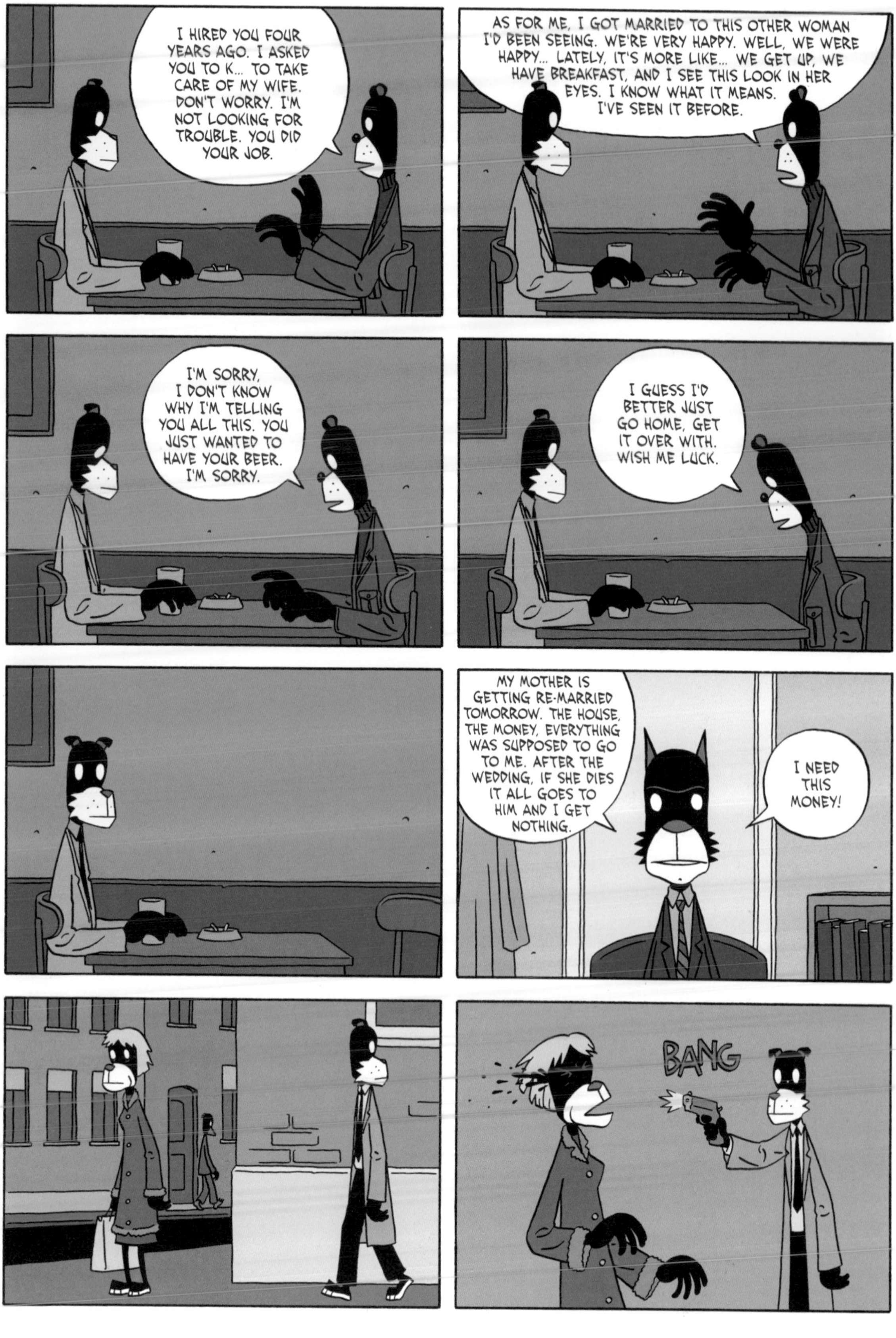
I HIRED YOU FOUR YEARS AGO. I ASKED YOU TO K... TO TAKE CARE OF MY WIFE. DON'T WORRY. I'M NOT LOOKING FOR TROUBLE. YOU DID YOUR JOB.
AS FOR ME, I GOT MARRIED TO THIS OTHER WOMAN I'D BEEN SEEING. WE'RE VERY HAPPY. WELL, WE WERE HAPPY... LATELY, IT'S MORE LIKE... WE GET UP, WE HAVE BREAKFAST, AND I SEE THIS LOOK IN HER EYES. I KNOW WHAT IT MEANS. I'VE SEEN IT BEFORE.
I'M SORRY, I DON'T KNOW WHY I'M TELLING YOU ALL THIS. YOU JUST WANTED TO HAVE YOUR BEER. I'M SORRY.
I GUESS I'D BETTER JUST GO HOME, GET IT OVER WITH. WISH ME LUCK.
MY MOTHER IS GETTING RE-MARRIED TOMORROW. THE HOUSE, THE MONEY, EVERYTHING WAS SUPPOSED TO GO TO ME. AFTER THE WEDDING, IF SHE DIES IT ALL GOES TO HIM AND I GET NOTHING.
I NEED THIS MONEY!
BANG

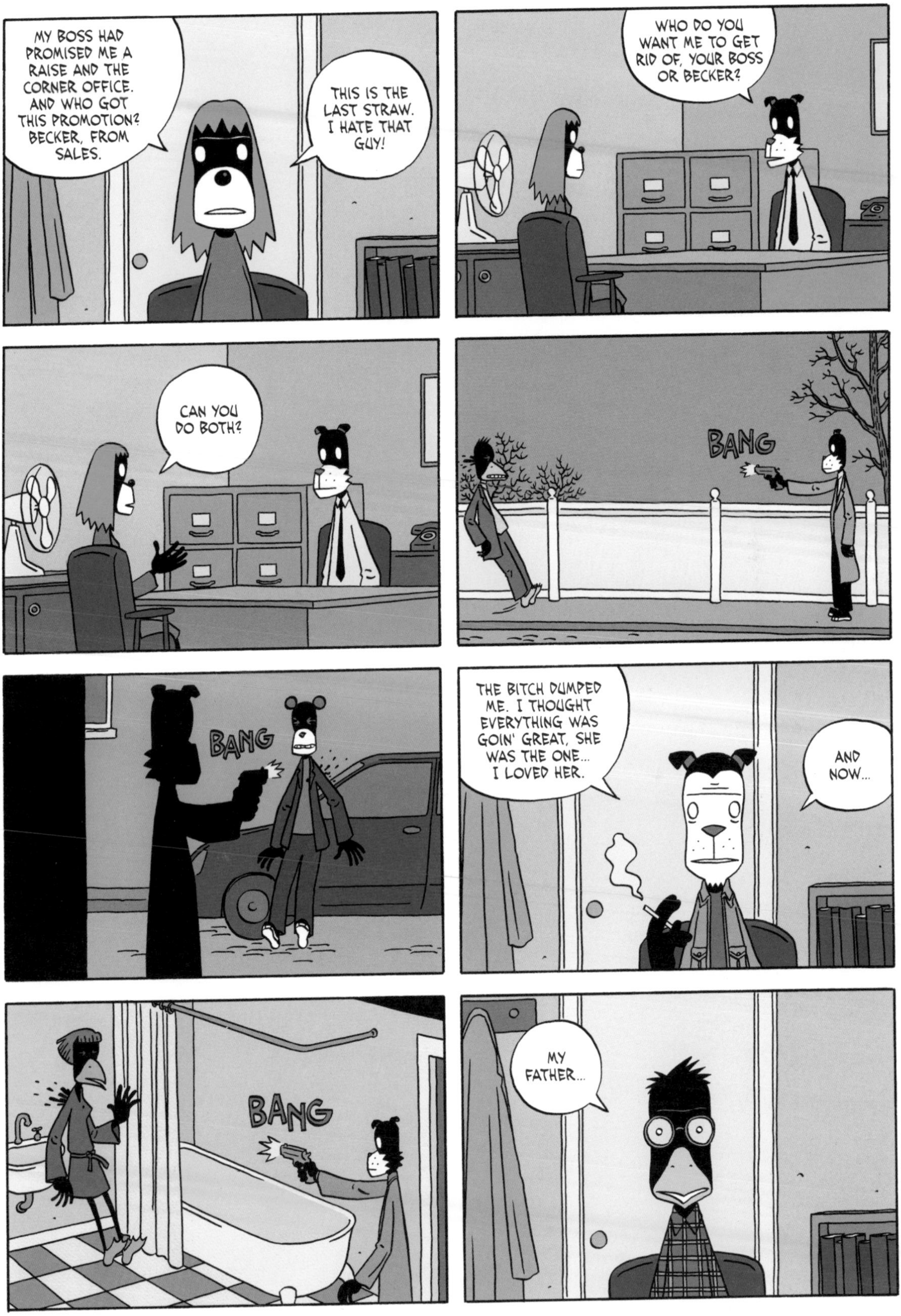
MY BOSS HAD PROMISED ME A RAISE AND THE CORNER OFFICE. AND WHO GOT THIS PROMOTION? BECKER, FROM SALES.
THIS IS THE LAST STRAW. I HATE THAT GUY!
WHO DO YOU WANT ME TO GET RID OF, YOUR BOSS OR BECKER?
CAN YOU DO BOTH?
BANG
BANG
THE BITCH DUMPED ME. I THOUGHT EVERYTHING WAS GOIN' GREAT, SHE WAS THE ONE... I LOVED HER.
AND NOW...
BANG
MY FATHER...

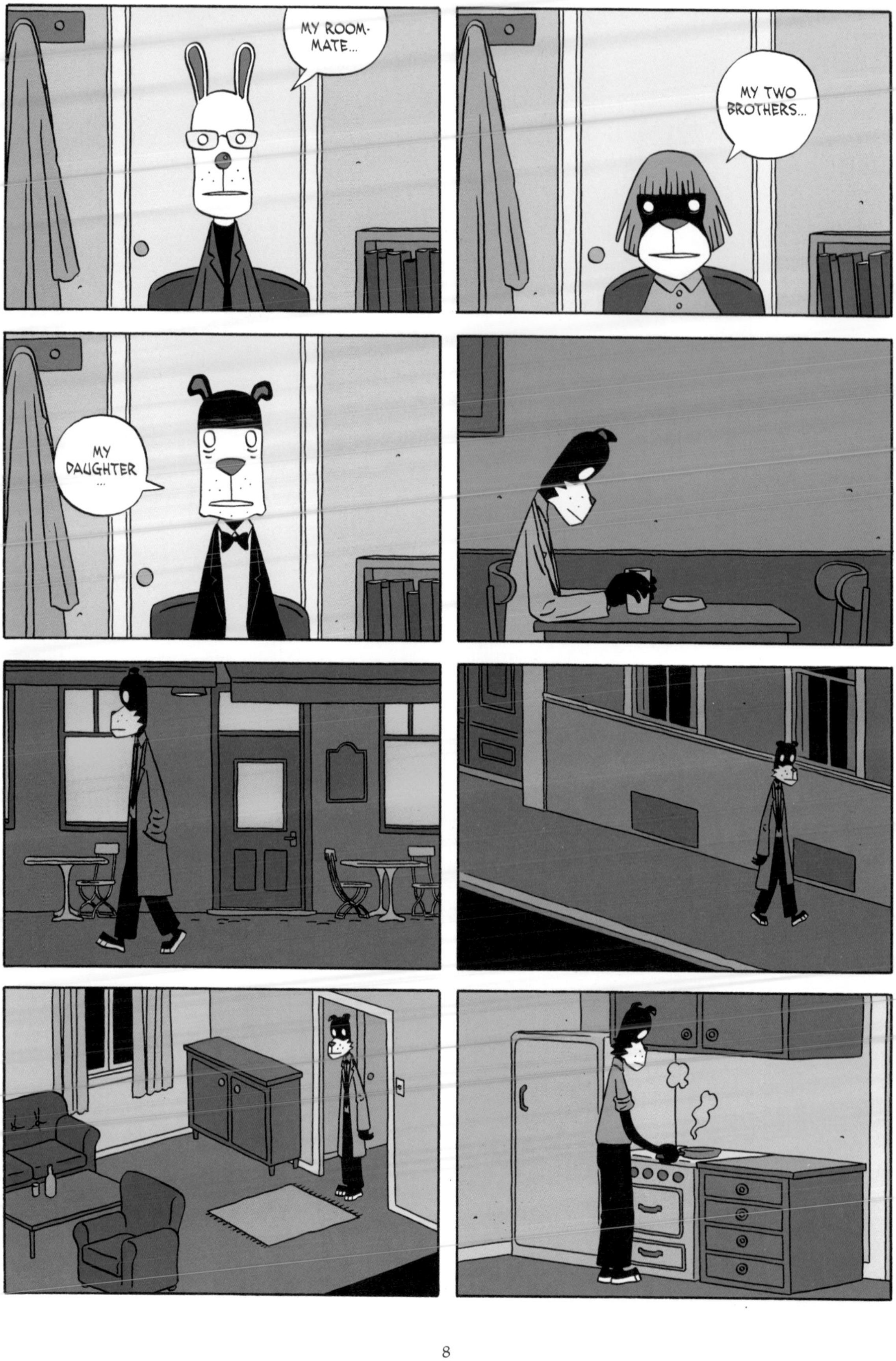
MY ROOM-
MATE...
MY TWO
BROTHERS...
MY
DAUGHTER
...

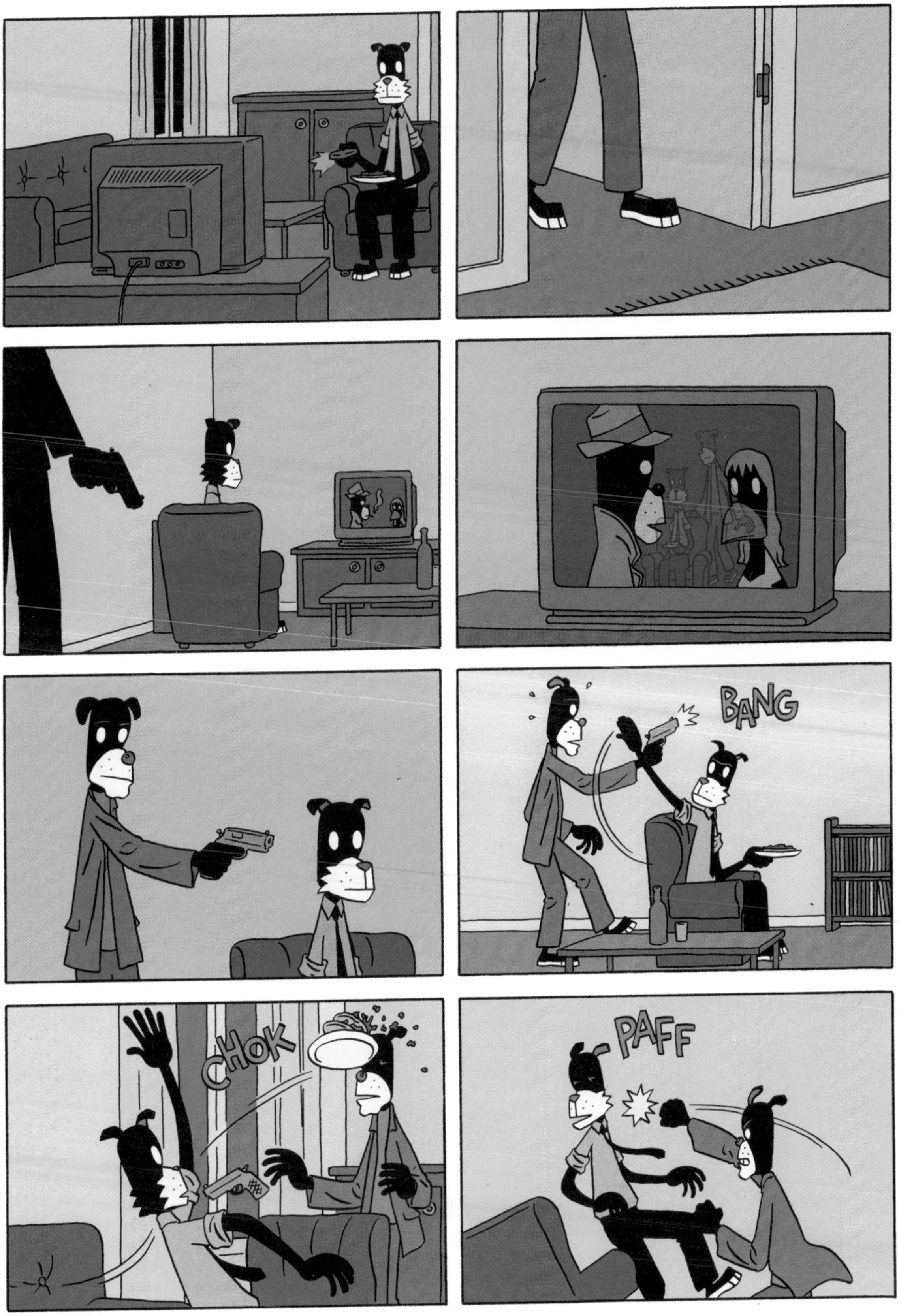
BANG
CHOK
PAFF

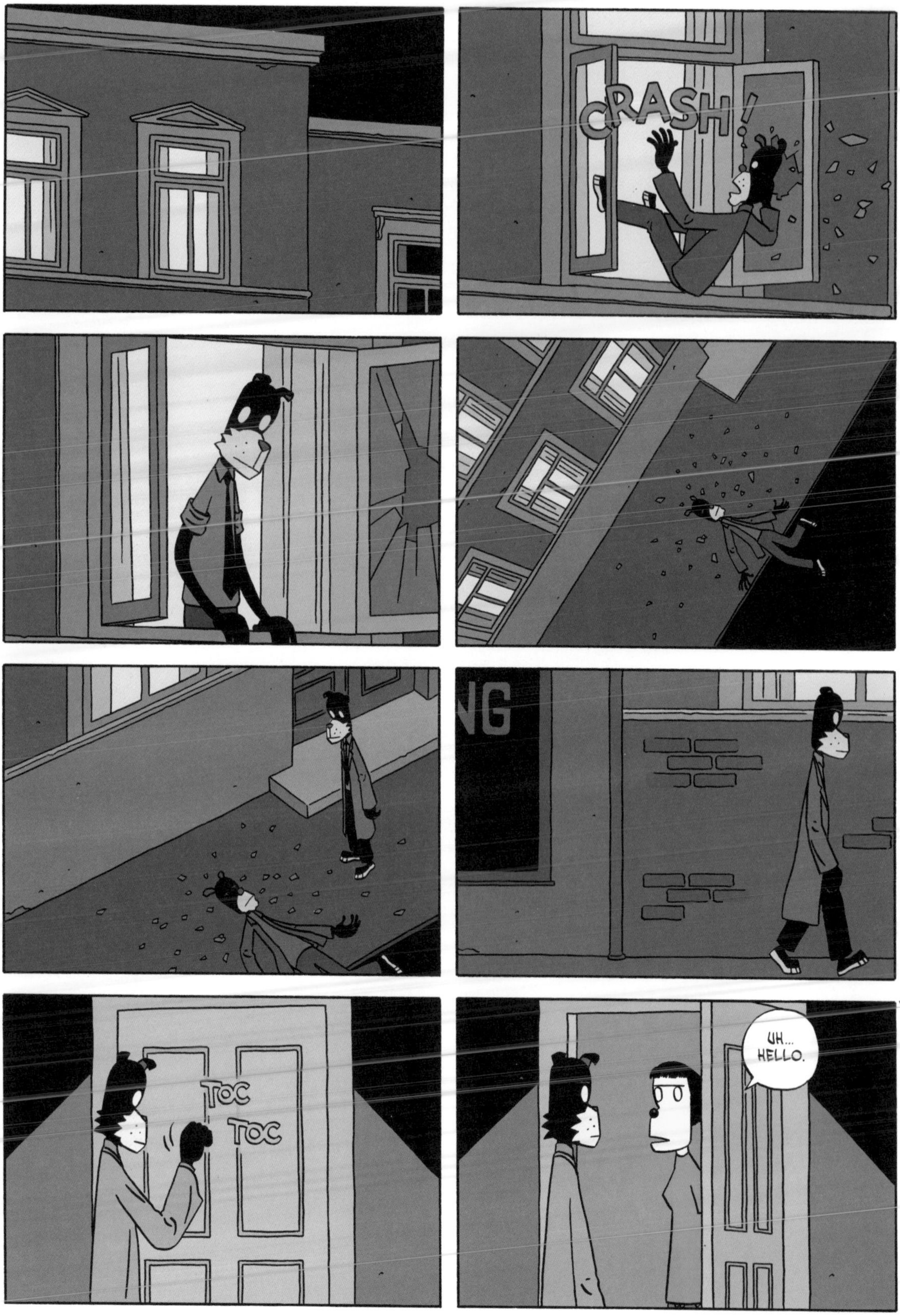
CRASH!
NG
TOC
TOC
UH...
HELLO.

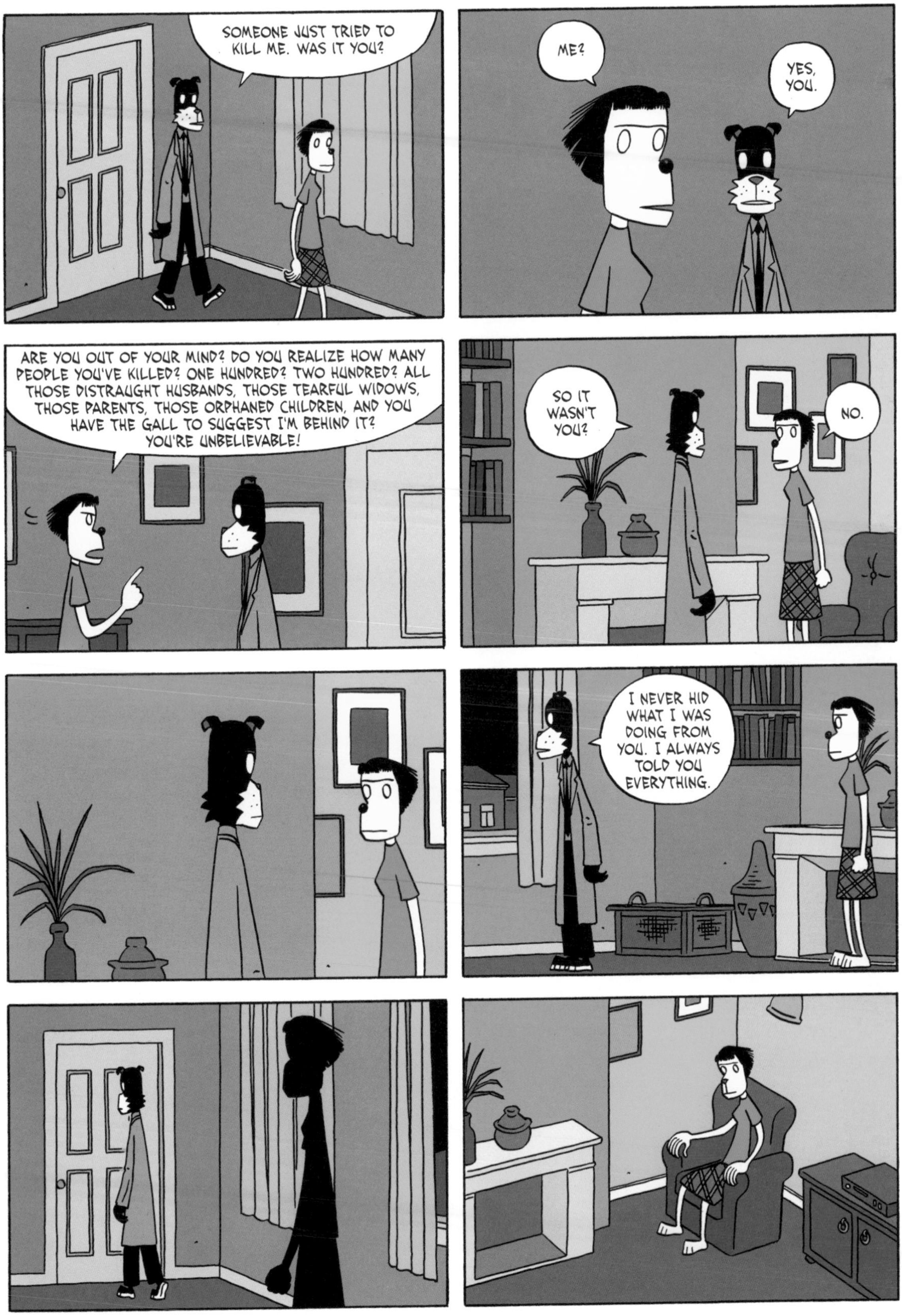
SOMEONE JUST TRIED TO KILL ME. WAS IT YOU?
ME?
YES, YOU.
ARE YOU OUT OF YOUR MIND? DO YOU REALIZE HOW MANY PEOPLE YOU'VE KILLED? ONE HUNDRED? TWO HUNDRED? ALL THOSE DISTRAUGHT HUSBANDS, THOSE TEARFUL WIDOWS, THOSE PARENTS, THOSE ORPHANED CHILDREN, AND YOU HAVE THE GALL TO SUGGEST I'M BEHIND IT? YOU'RE UNBELIEVABLE!
SO IT WASN'T YOU?
NO.
I NEVER HID WHAT I WAS DOING FROM YOU. I ALWAYS TOLD YOU EVERYTHING.

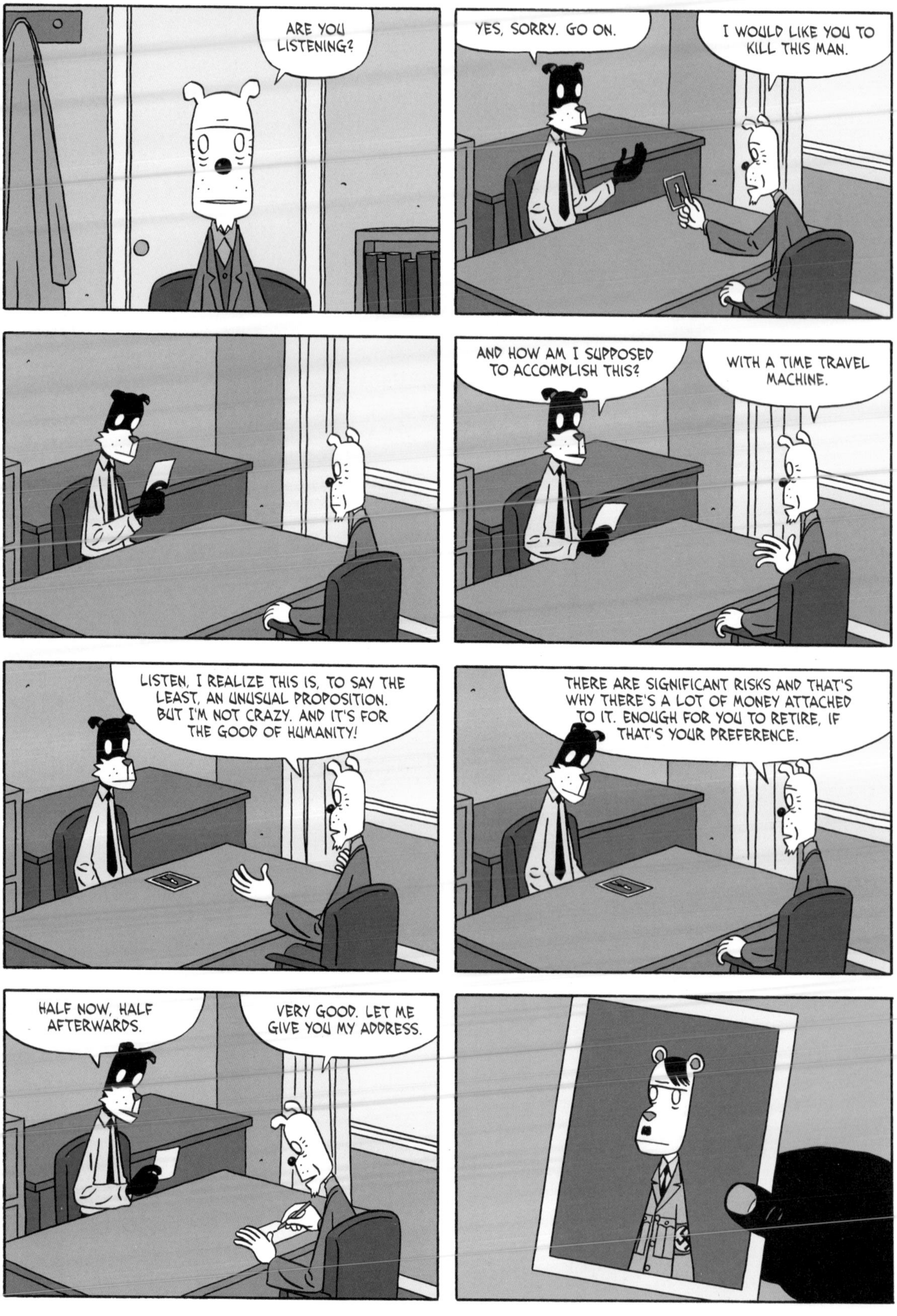
ARE YOU LISTENING?
YES, SORRY. GO ON.
I WOULD LIKE YOU TO KILL THIS MAN.
AND HOW AM I SUPPOSED TO ACCOMPLISH THIS?
WITH A TIME TRAVEL MACHINE.
LISTEN, I REALIZE THIS IS, TO SAY THE LEAST, AN UNUSUAL PROPOSITION. BUT I'M NOT CRAZY. AND IT'S FOR THE GOOD OF HUMANITY!
THERE ARE SIGNIFICANT RISKS AND THAT'S WHY THERE'S A LOT OF MONEY ATTACHED TO IT. ENOUGH FOR YOU TO RETIRE, IF THAT'S YOUR PREFERENCE.
HALF NOW, HALF AFTERWARDS.
VERY GOOD. LET ME GIVE YOU MY ADDRESS.

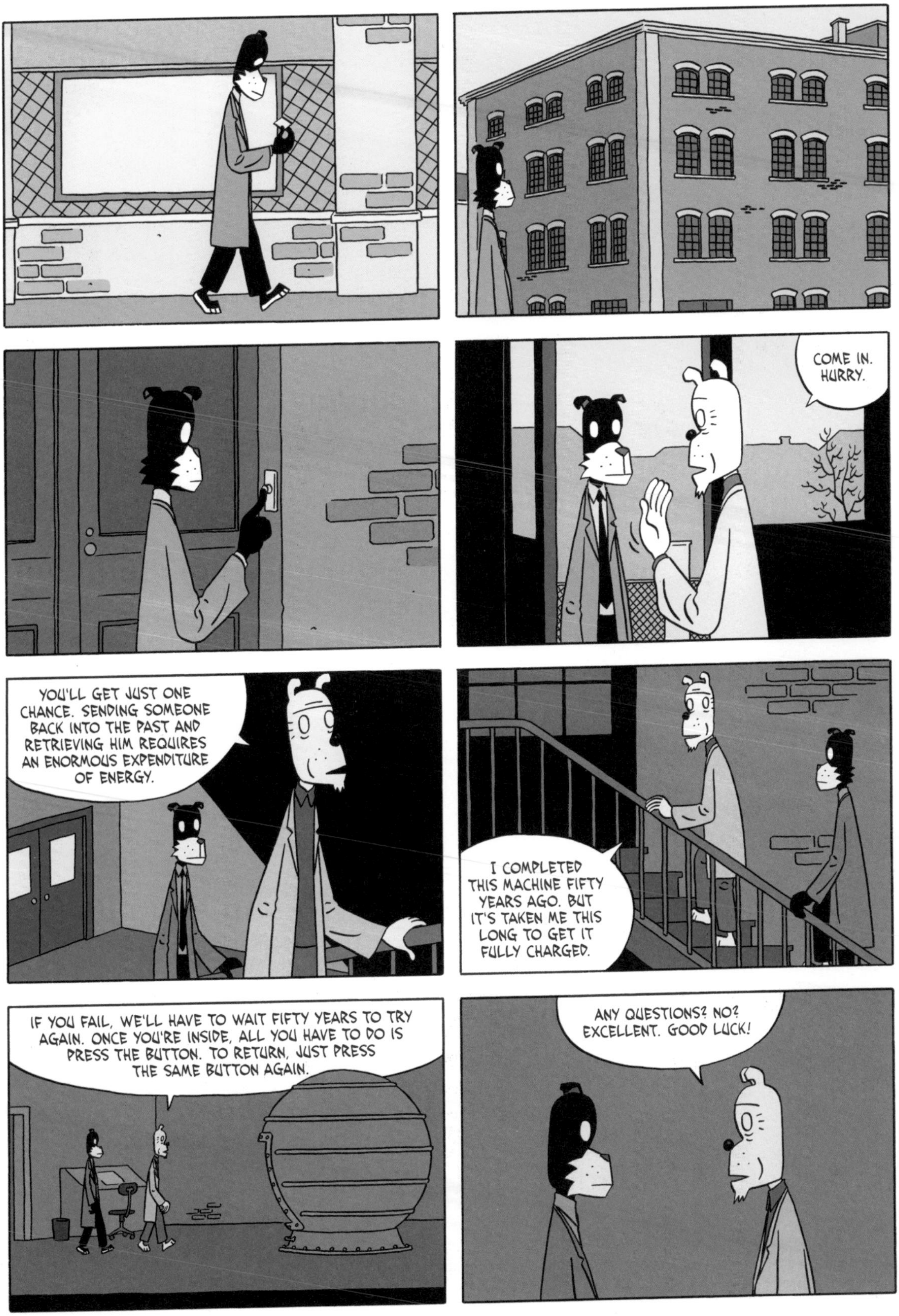
COME IN. HURRY.
YOU'LL GET JUST ONE CHANCE. SENDING SOMEONE BACK INTO THE PAST AND RETRIEVING HIM REQUIRES AN ENORMOUS EXPENDITURE OF ENERGY.
I COMPLETED THIS MACHINE FIFTY YEARS AGO. BUT IT'S TAKEN ME THIS LONG TO GET IT FULLY CHARGED.
IF YOU FAIL, WE'LL HAVE TO WAIT FIFTY YEARS TO TRY AGAIN. ONCE YOU'RE INSIDE, ALL YOU HAVE TO DO IS PRESS THE BUTTON. TO RETURN, JUST PRESS THE SAME BUTTON AGAIN.
ANY QUESTIONS? NO? EXCELLENT. GOOD LUCK!

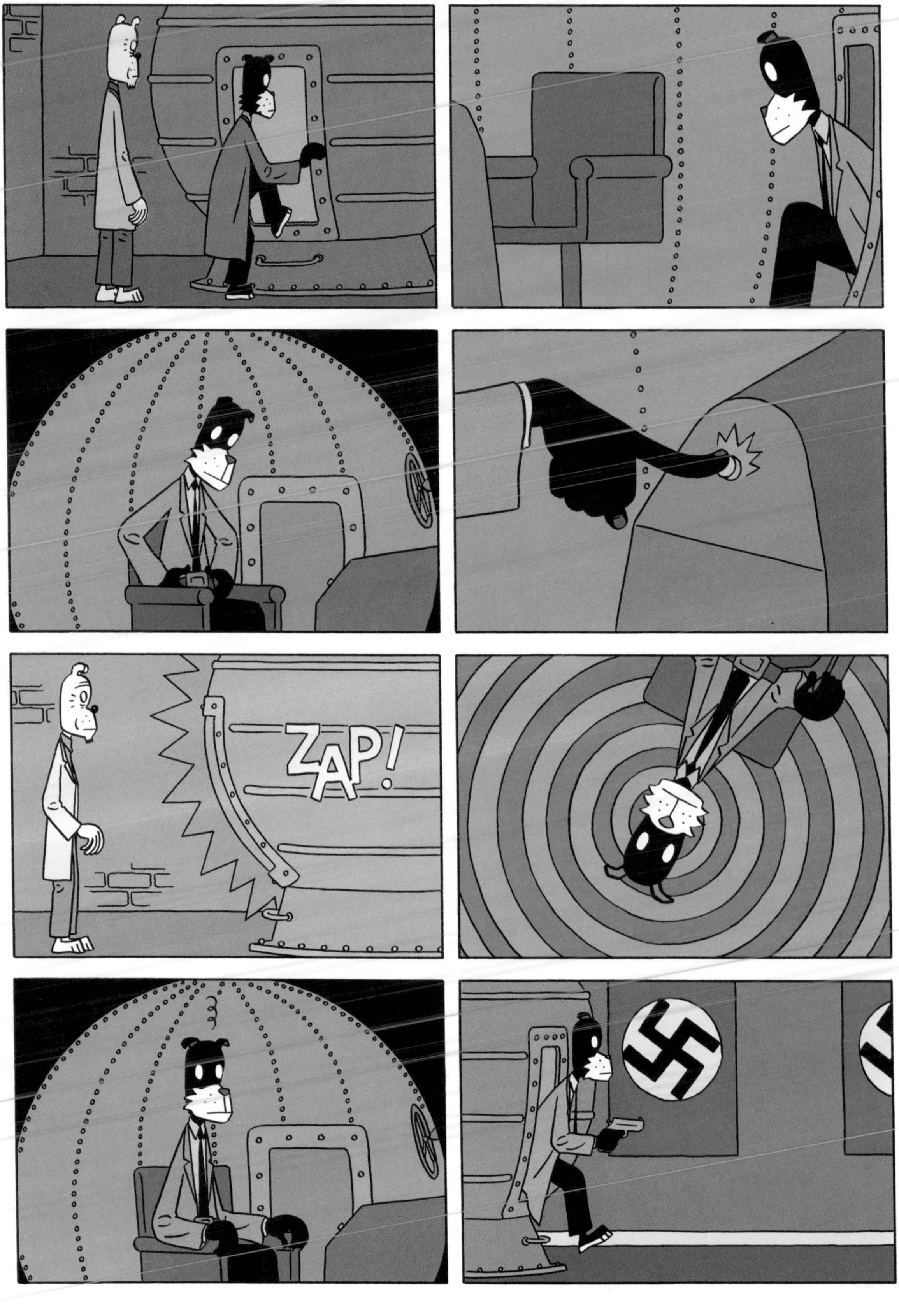
ZAP!

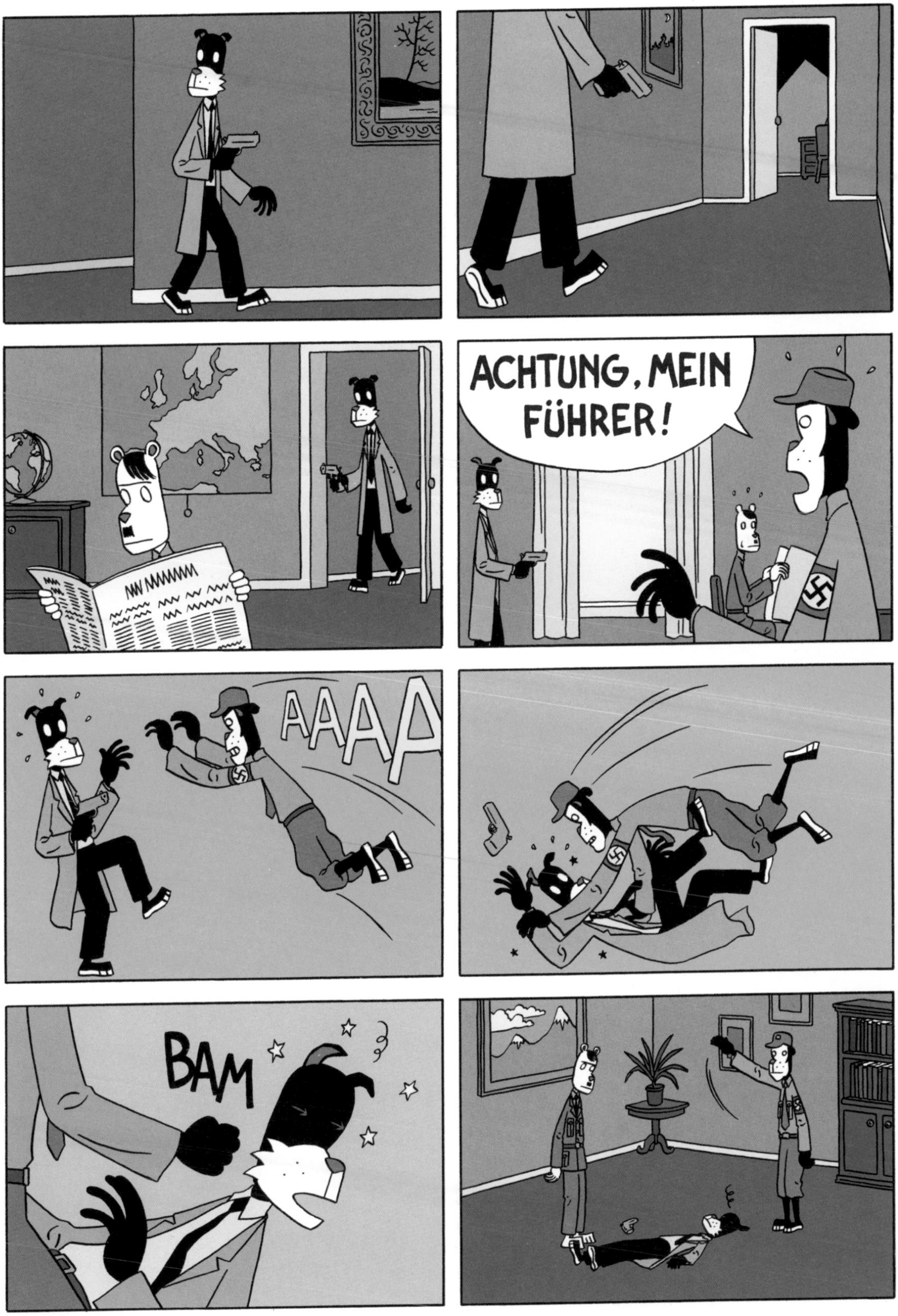
ACHTUNG, MEIN FÜHRER!
AAAA
BAM

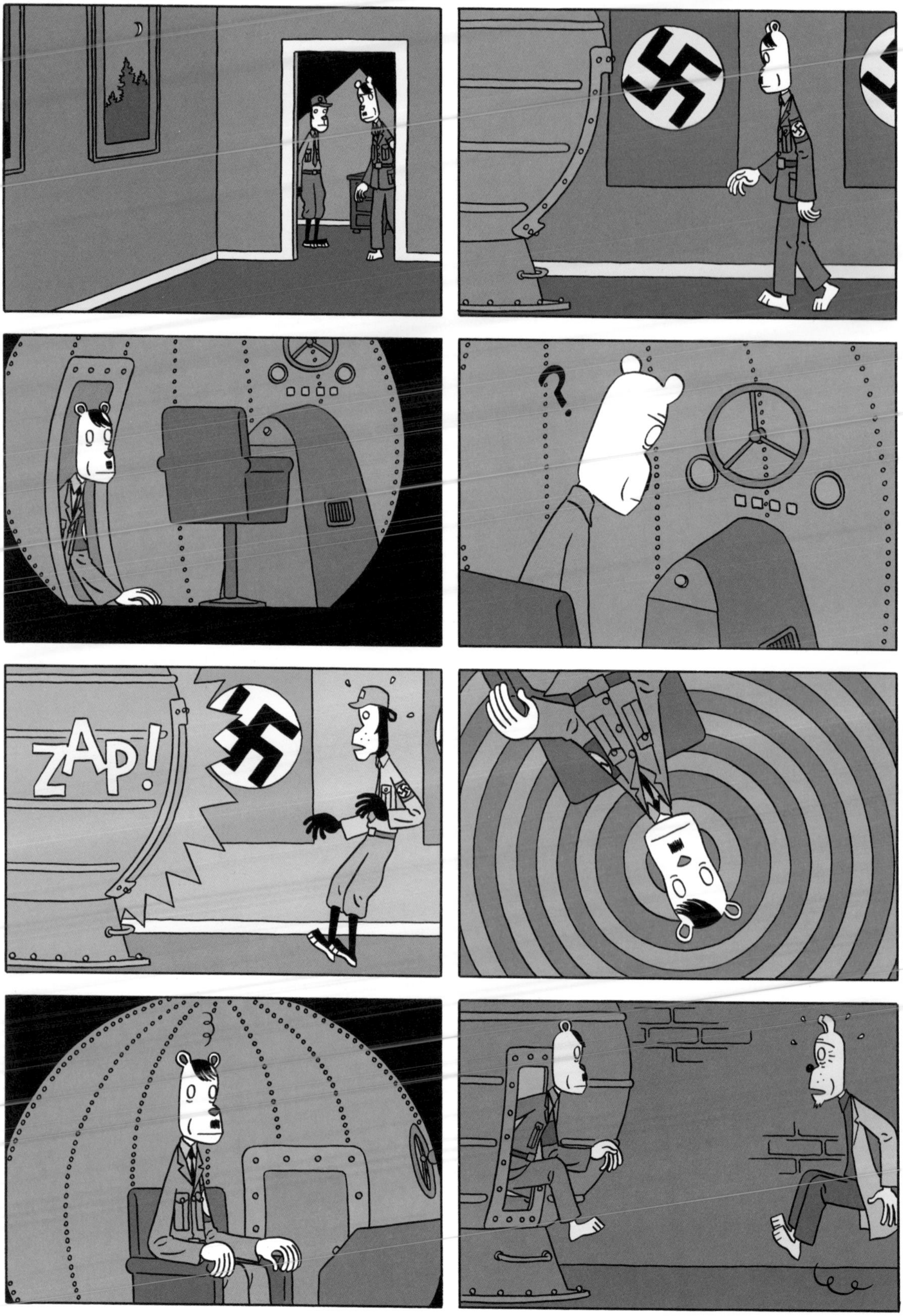
?
ZAP!

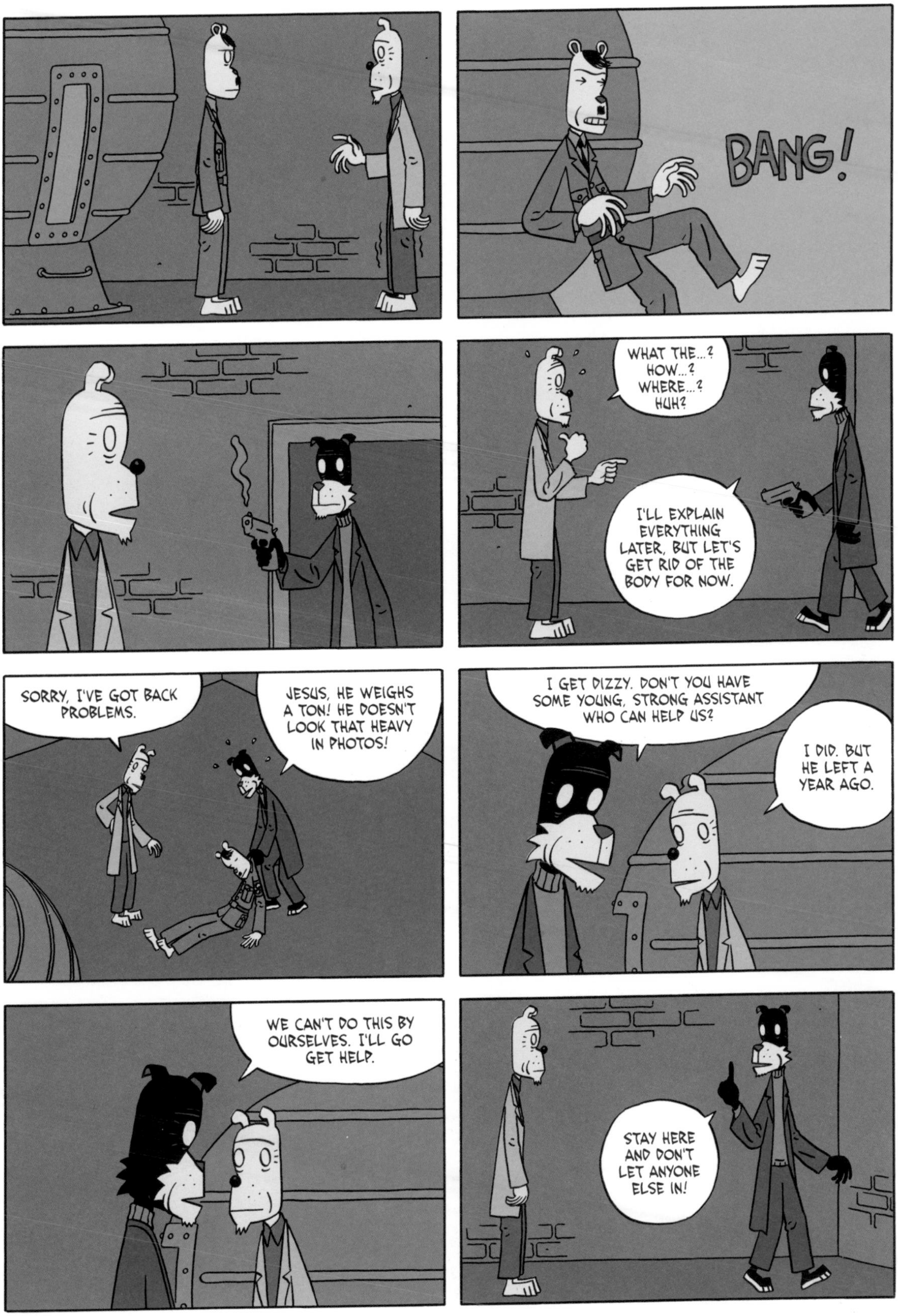
BANG!
WHAT THE...? HOW...? WHERE...? HUH?
I'LL EXPLAIN EVERYTHING LATER, BUT LET'S GET RID OF THE BODY FOR NOW.
SORRY, I'VE GOT BACK PROBLEMS.
JESUS, HE WEIGHS A TON! HE DOESN'T LOOK THAT HEAVY IN PHOTOS!
I GET DIZZY. DON'T YOU HAVE SOME YOUNG, STRONG ASSISTANT WHO CAN HELP US?
I DID. BUT HE LEFT A YEAR AGO.
WE CAN'T DO THIS BY OURSELVES. I'LL GO GET HELP.
STAY HERE AND DON'T LET ANYONE ELSE IN!

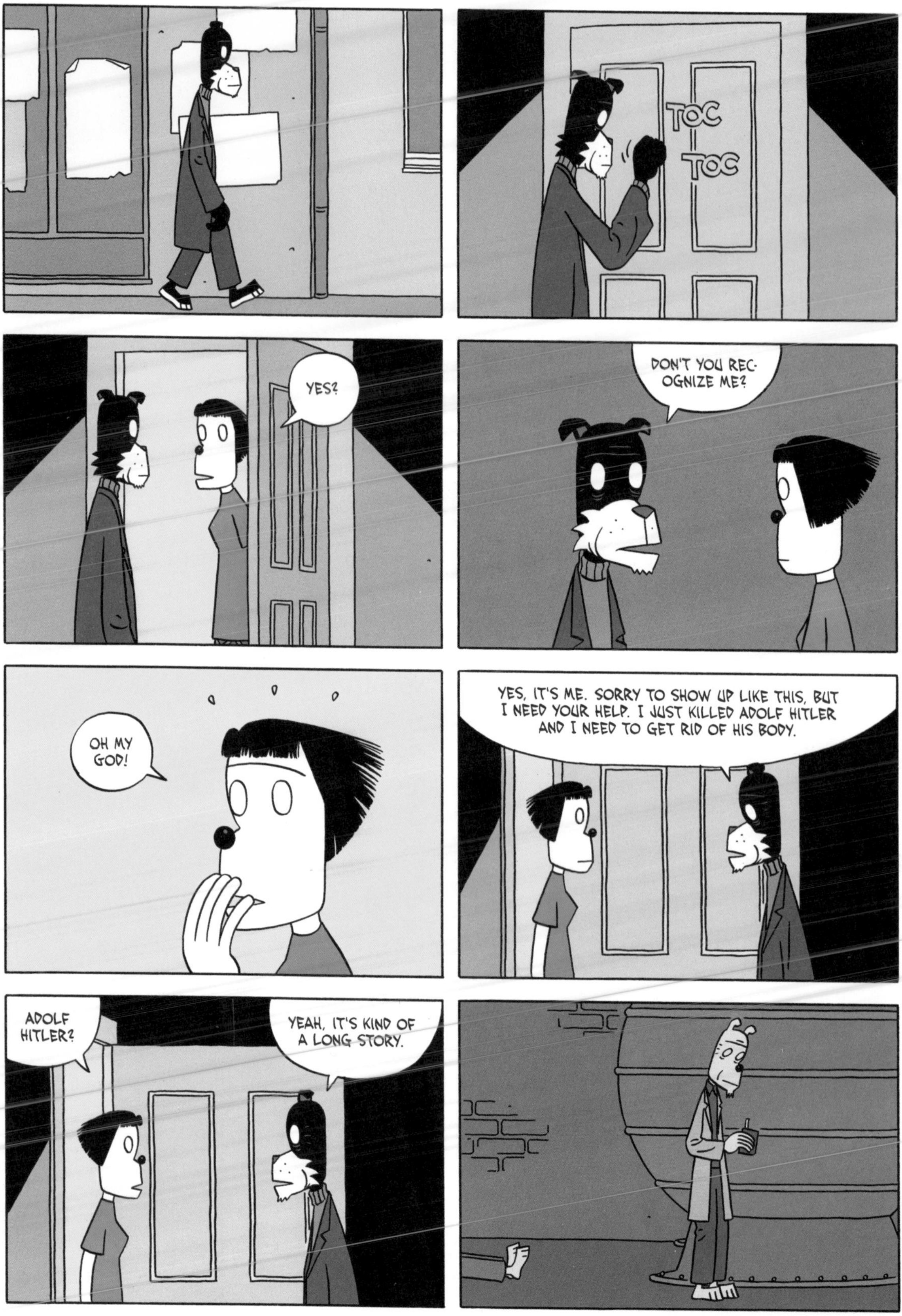
TOC
TOC
YES?
DON'T YOU REC-
OGNIZE ME?
OH MY
GOD!
YES, IT'S ME. SORRY TO SHOW UP LIKE THIS, BUT
I NEED YOUR HELP. I JUST KILLED ADOLF HITLER
AND I NEED TO GET RID OF HIS BODY.
ADOLF
HITLER?
YEAH, IT'S KIND OF
A LONG STORY.

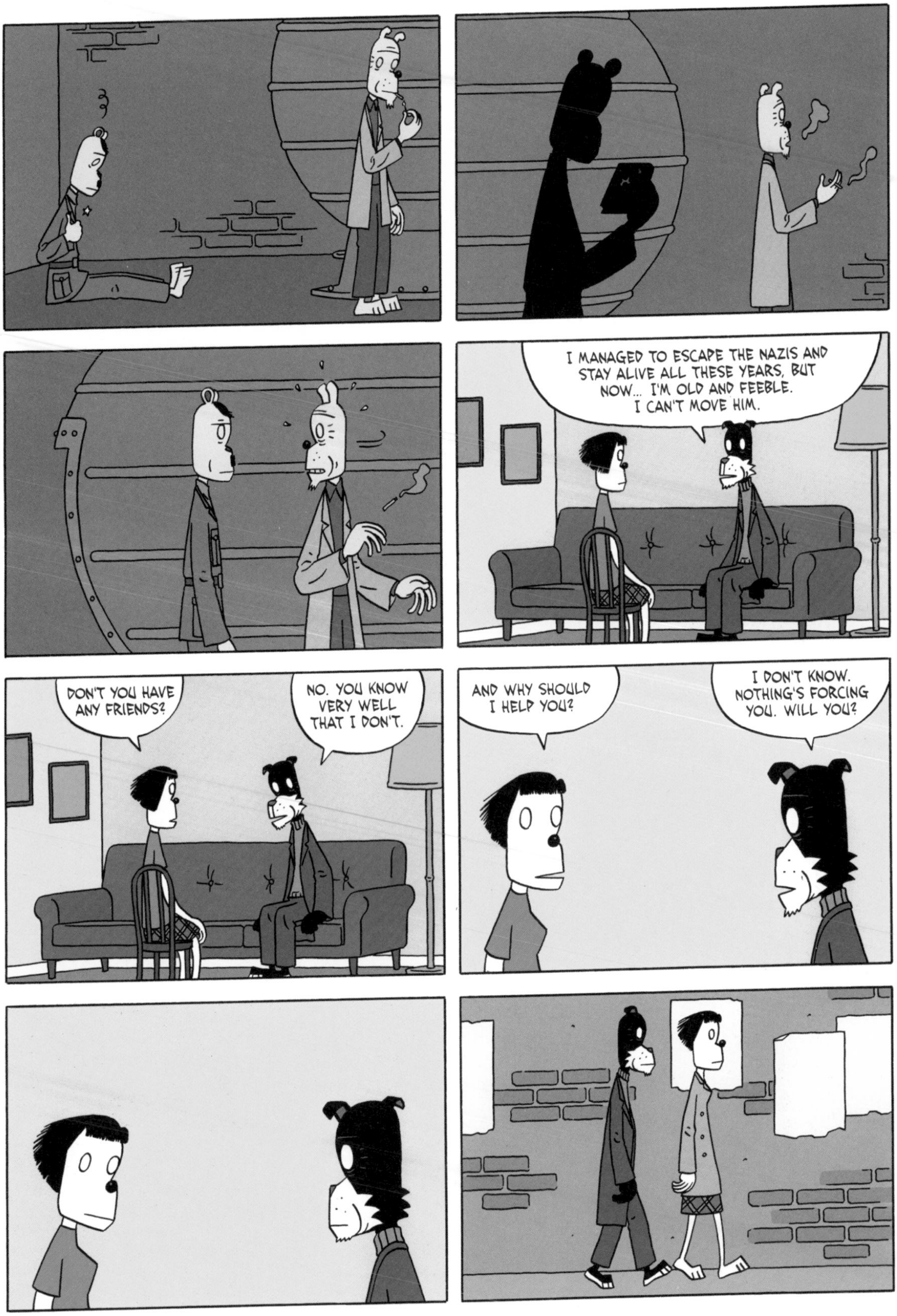
I MANAGED TO ESCAPE THE NAZIS AND STAY ALIVE ALL THESE YEARS, BUT NOW... I'M OLD AND FEEBLE. I CAN'T MOVE HIM.
DON'T YOU HAVE ANY FRIENDS?
NO. YOU KNOW VERY WELL THAT I DON'T.
AND WHY SHOULD I HELP YOU?
I DON'T KNOW. NOTHING'S FORCING YOU. WILL YOU?

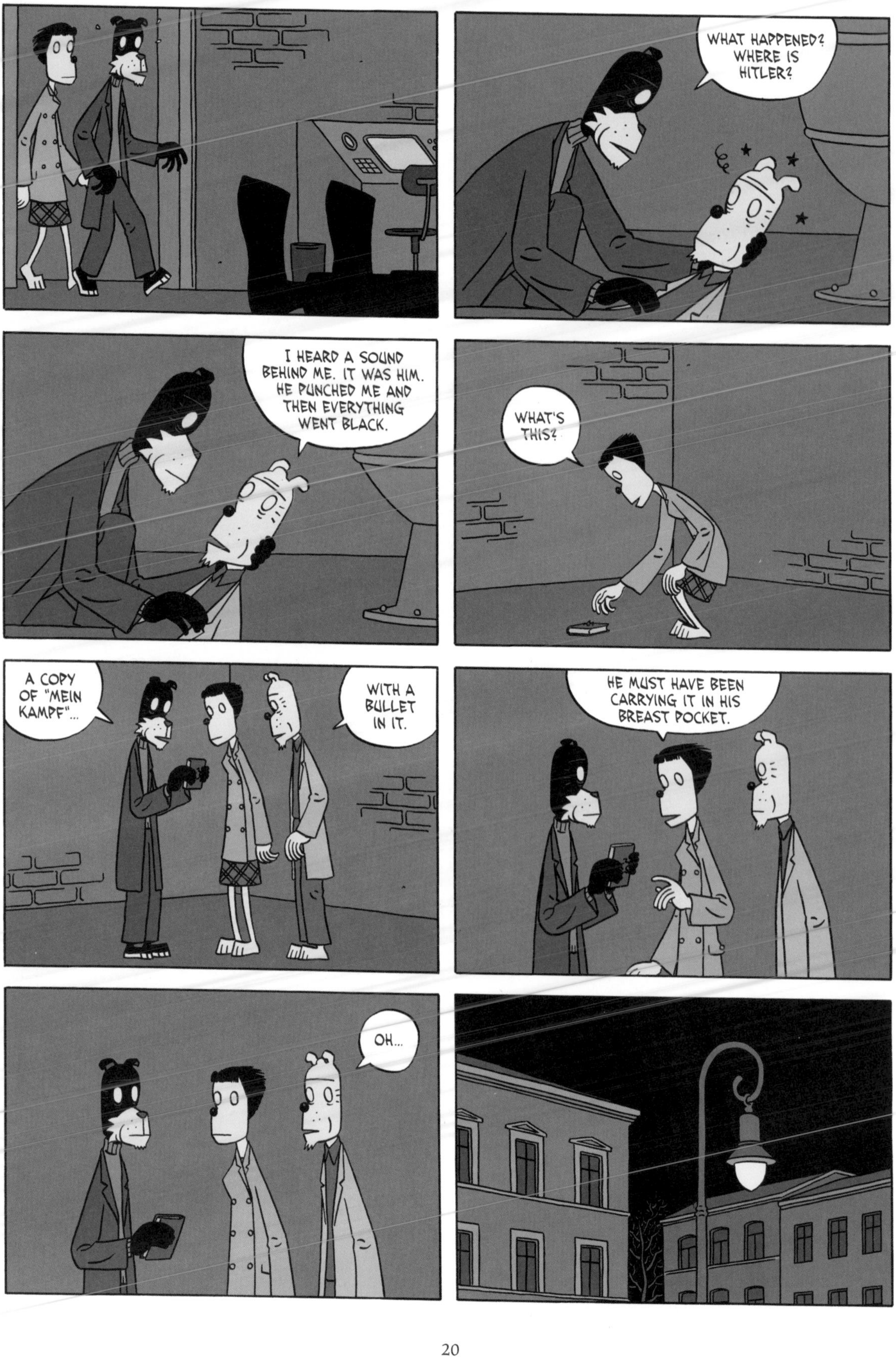
WHAT HAPPENED? WHERE IS HITLER?
I HEARD A SOUND BEHIND ME. IT WAS HIM. HE PUNCHED ME AND THEN EVERYTHING WENT BLACK.
WHAT'S THIS?
A COPY OF "MEIN KAMPF"...
WITH A BULLET IN IT.
HE MUST HAVE BEEN CARRYING IT IN HIS BREAST POCKET.
OH...

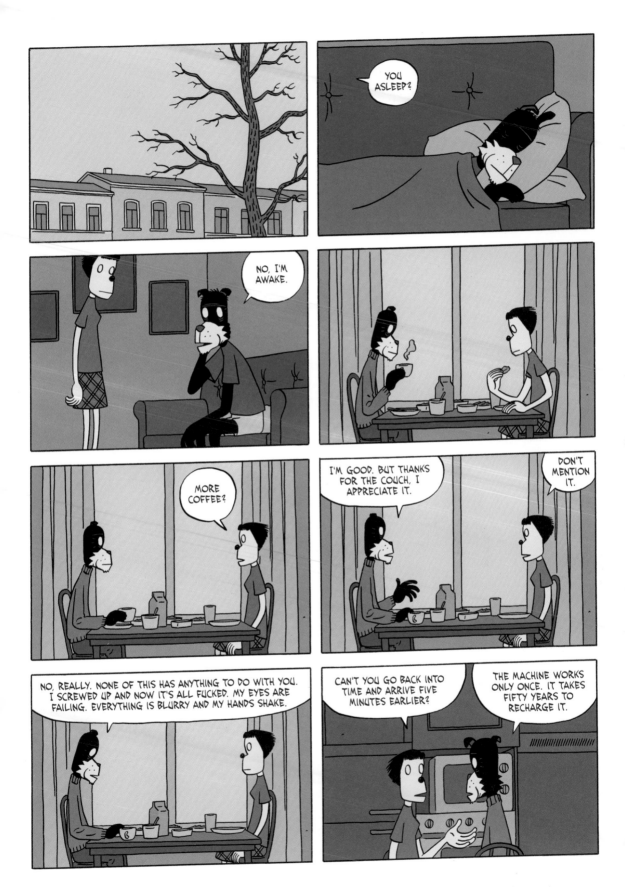

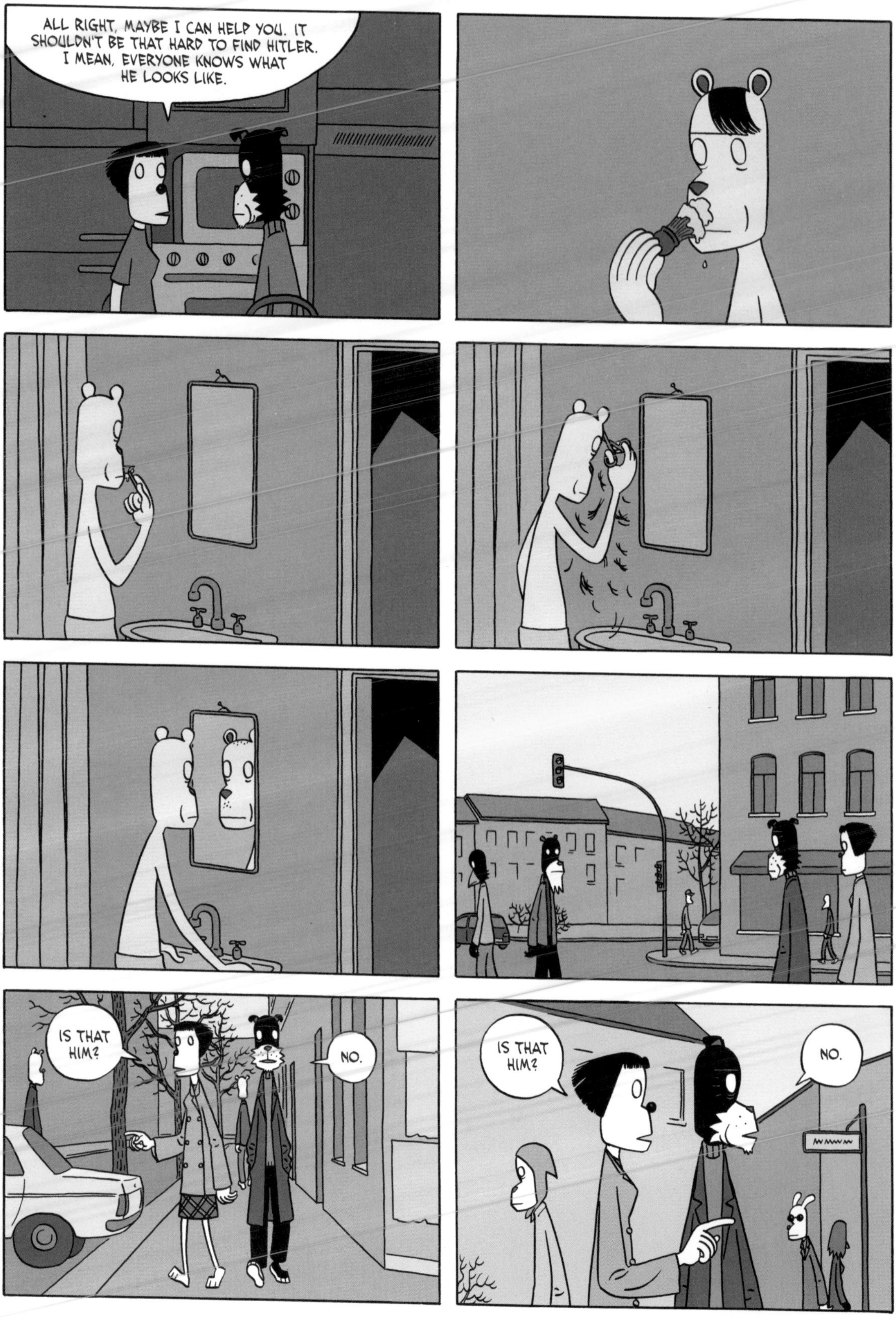
ALL RIGHT, MAYBE I CAN HELP YOU. IT SHOULDN'T BE THAT HARD TO FIND HITLER. I MEAN, EVERYONE KNOWS WHAT HE LOOKS LIKE.
IS THAT HIM?
NO.
IS THAT HIM?
NO.

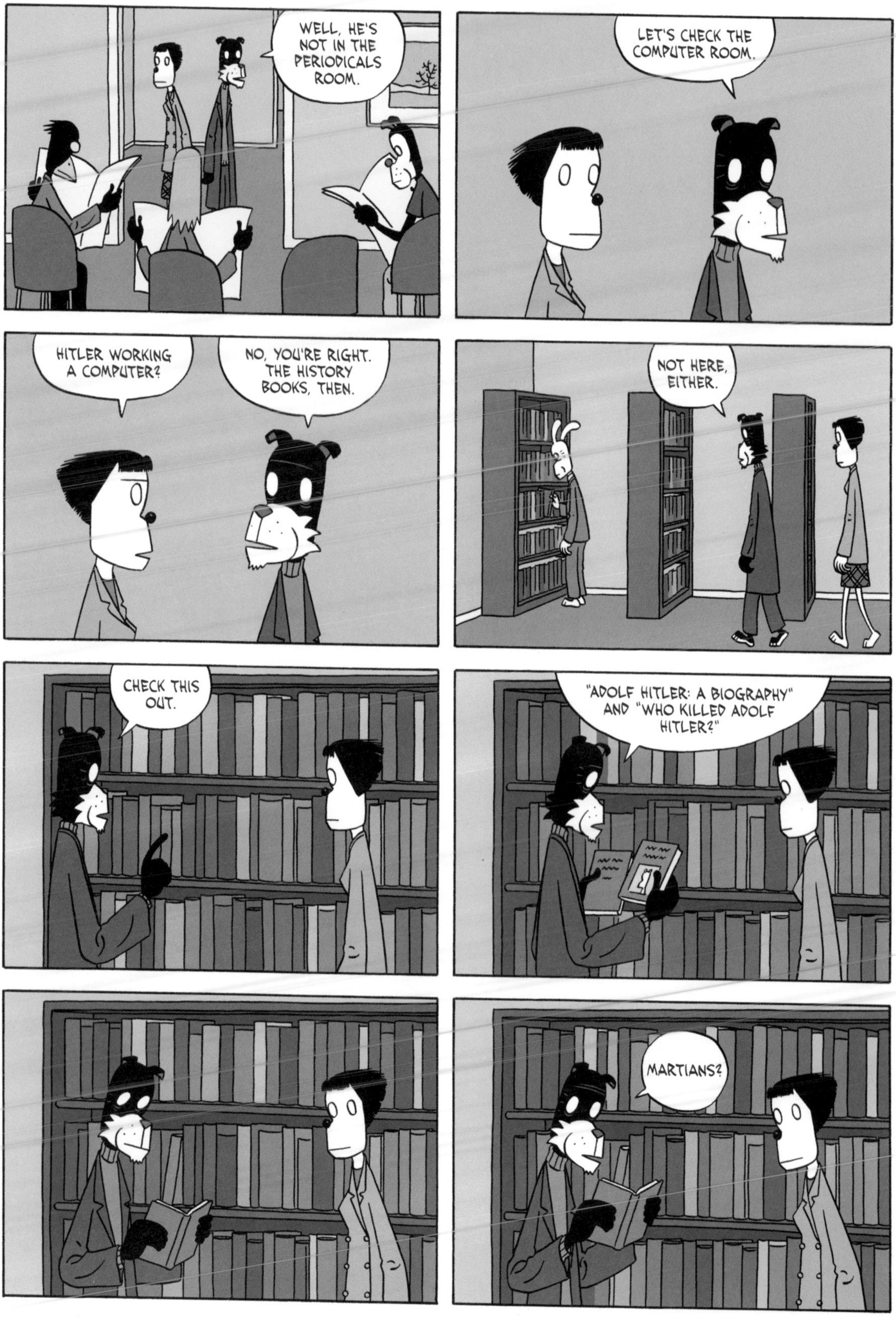
WELL, HE'S NOT IN THE PERIODICALS ROOM.
LET'S CHECK THE COMPUTER ROOM.
HITLER WORKING A COMPUTER?
NO, YOU'RE RIGHT. THE HISTORY BOOKS, THEN.
NOT HERE, EITHER.
CHECK THIS OUT.
"ADOLF HITLER: A BIOGRAPHY" AND "WHO KILLED ADOLF HITLER?"
MARTIANS?

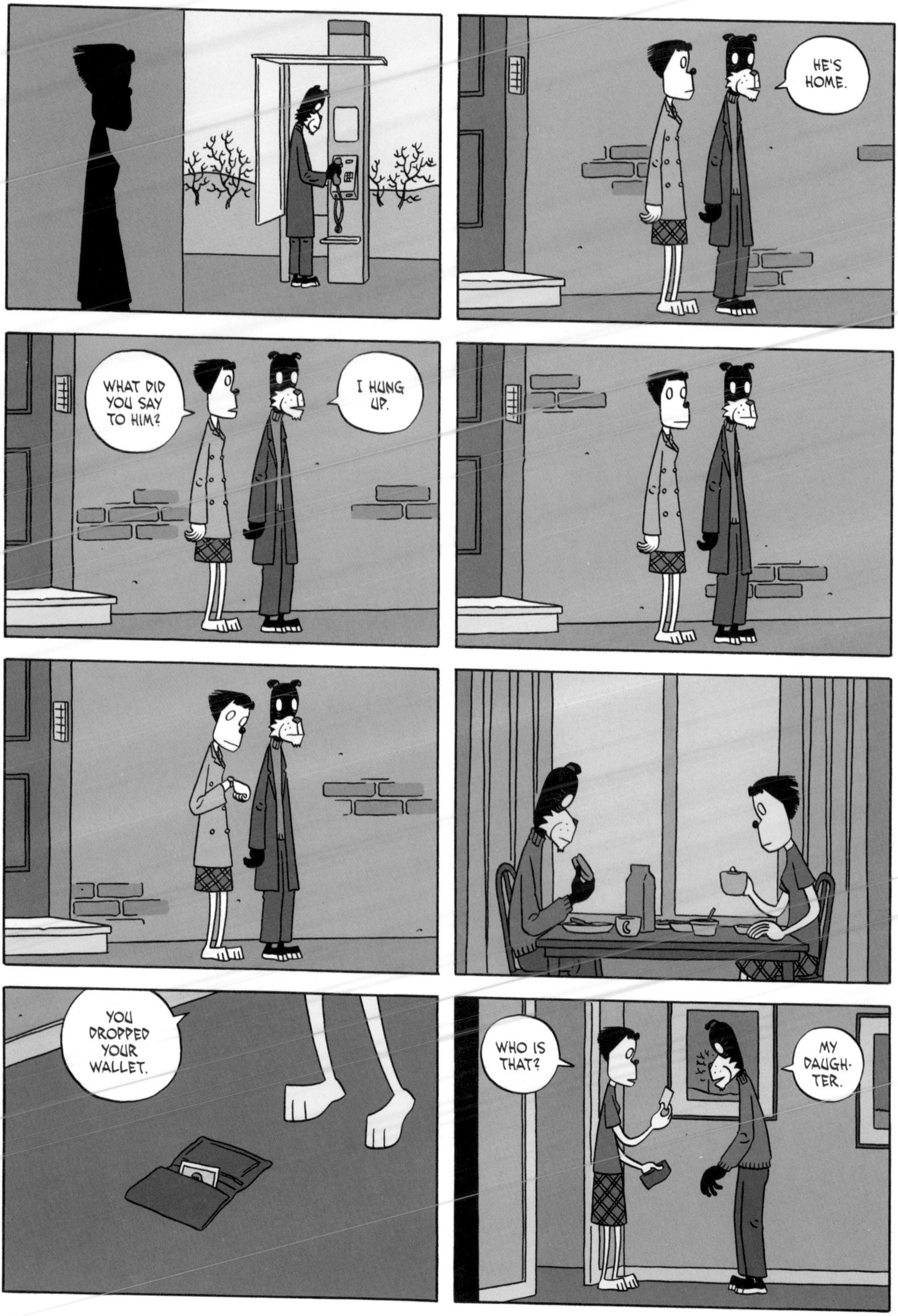

HE'S HOME.
WHAT DID YOU SAY TO HIM?
I HUNG UP.
YOU DROPPED YOUR WALLET.
WHO IS THAT?
MY DAUGH-TER.

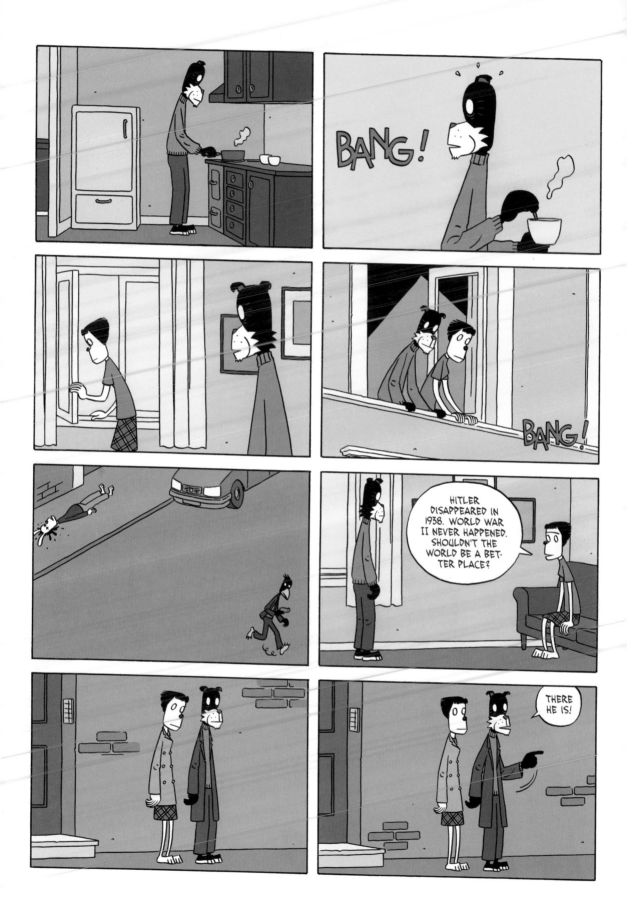

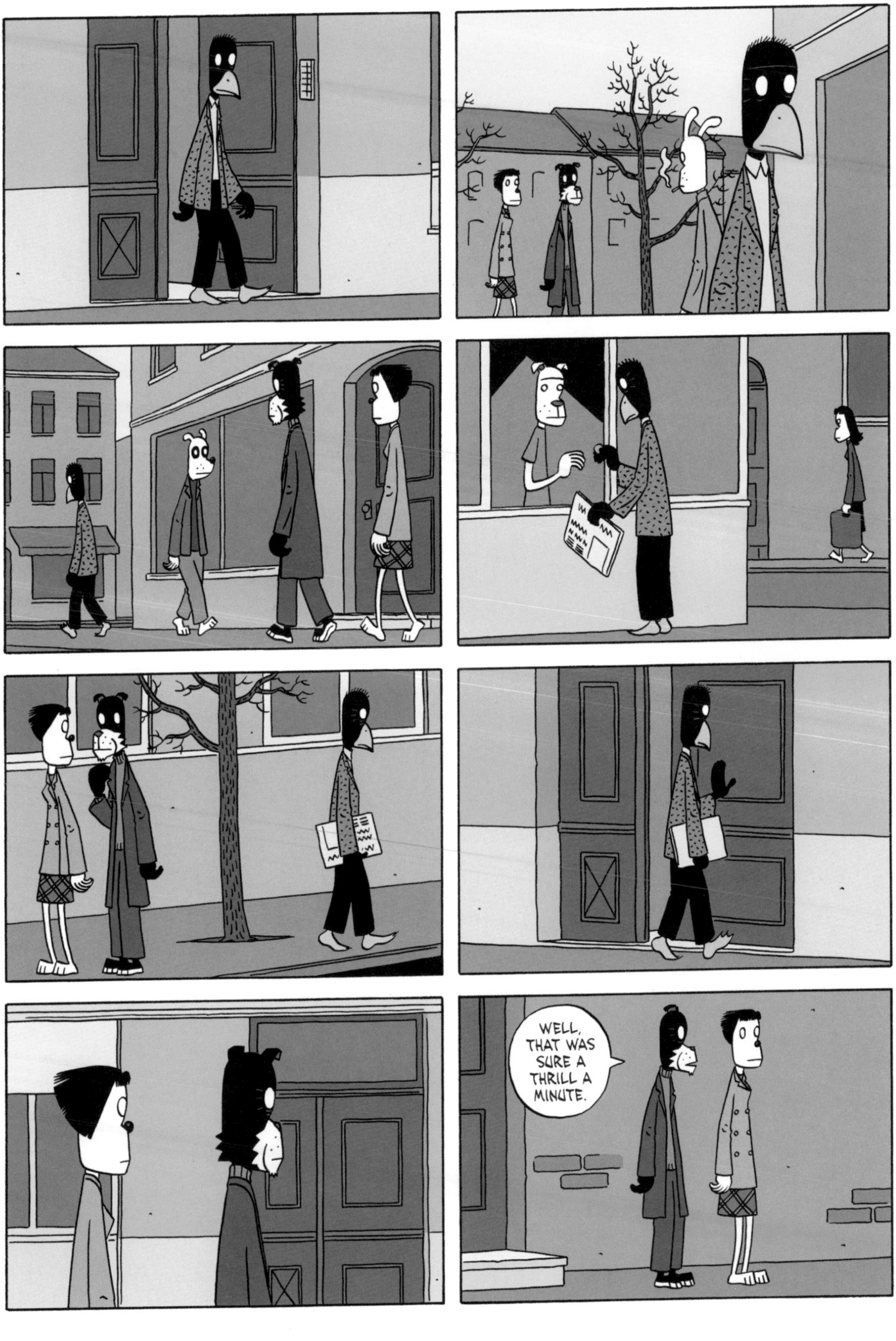
WELL, THAT WAS SURE A THRILL A MINUTE.

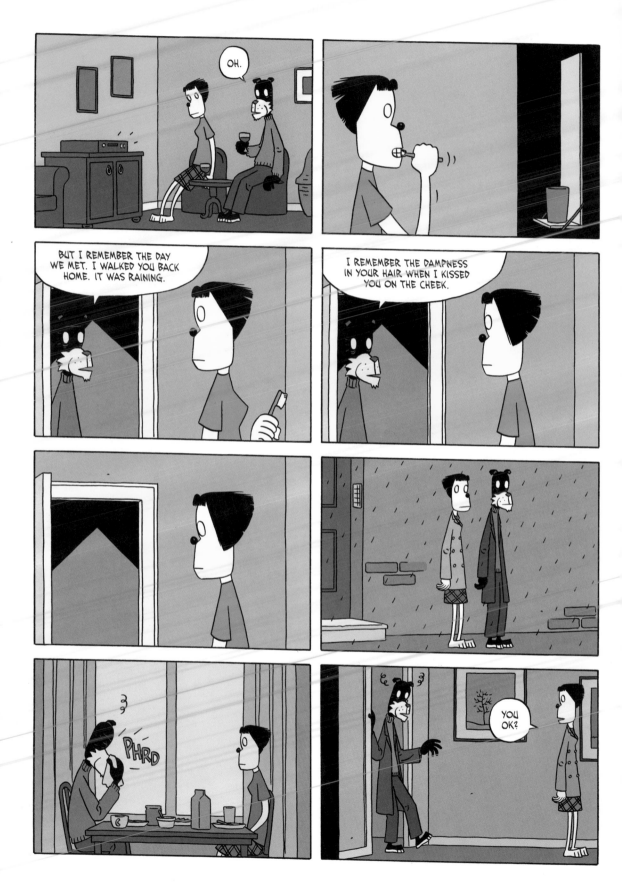

34

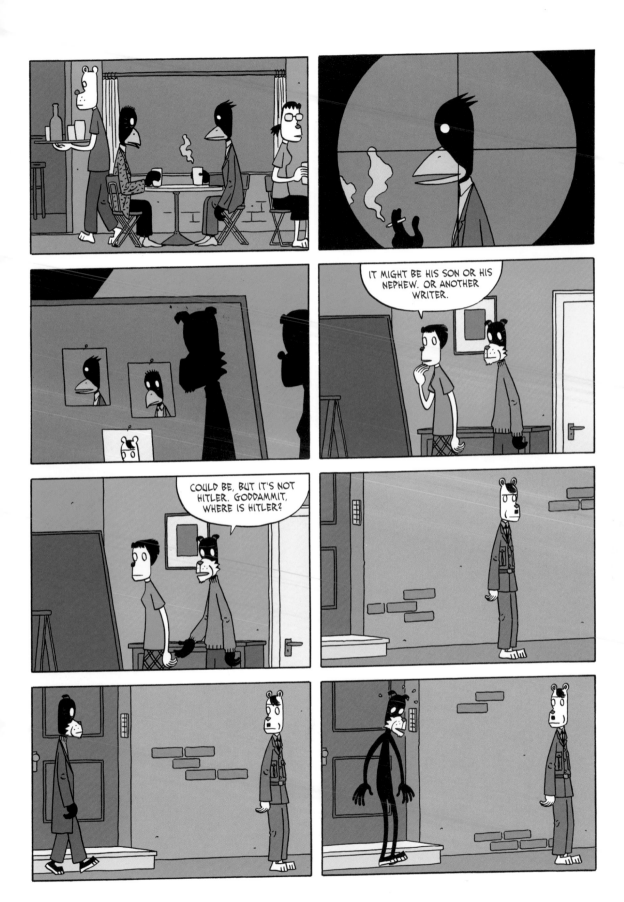

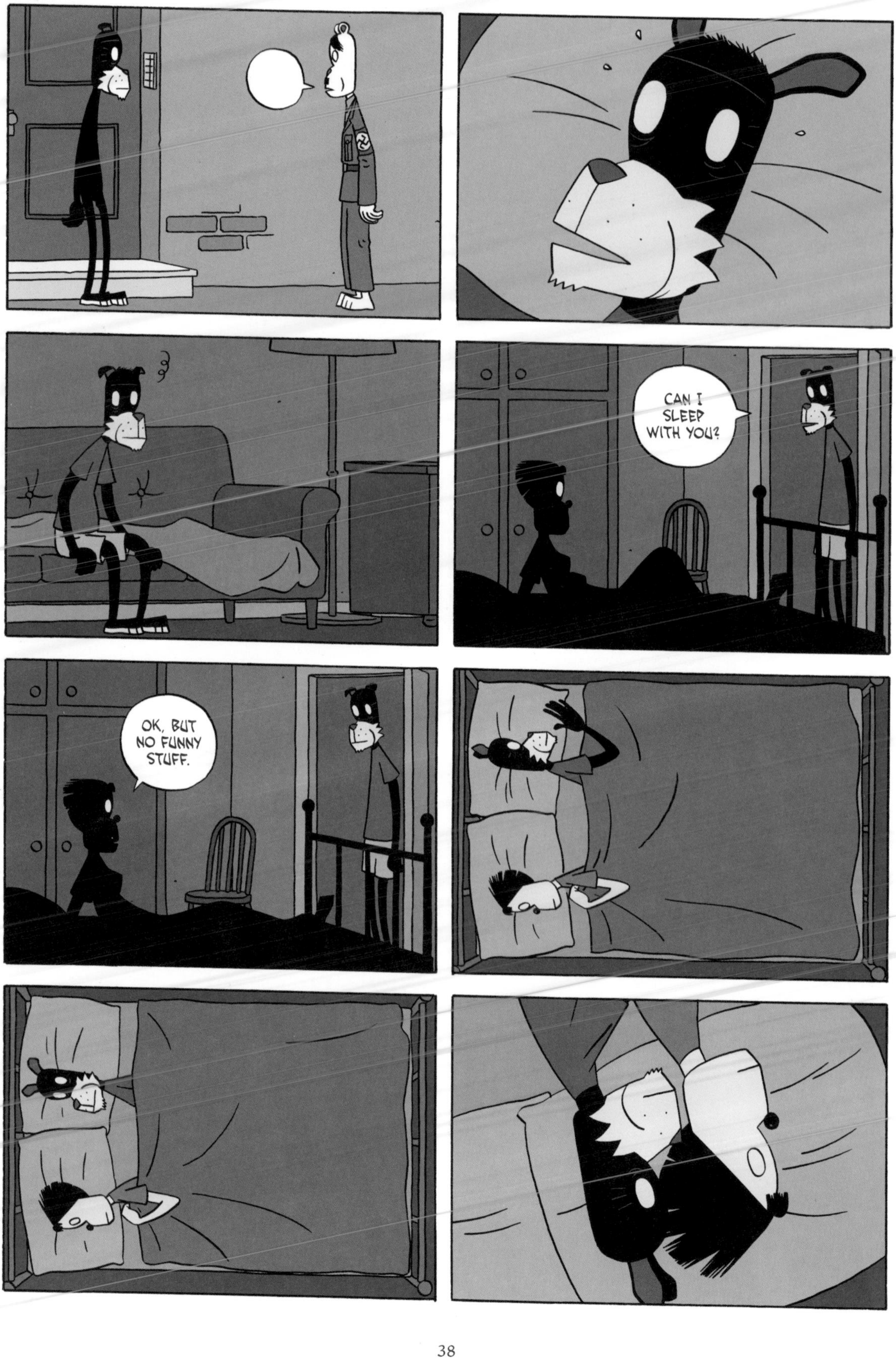
CAN I SLEEP WITH YOU?
OK, BUT NO FUNNY STUFF.

40

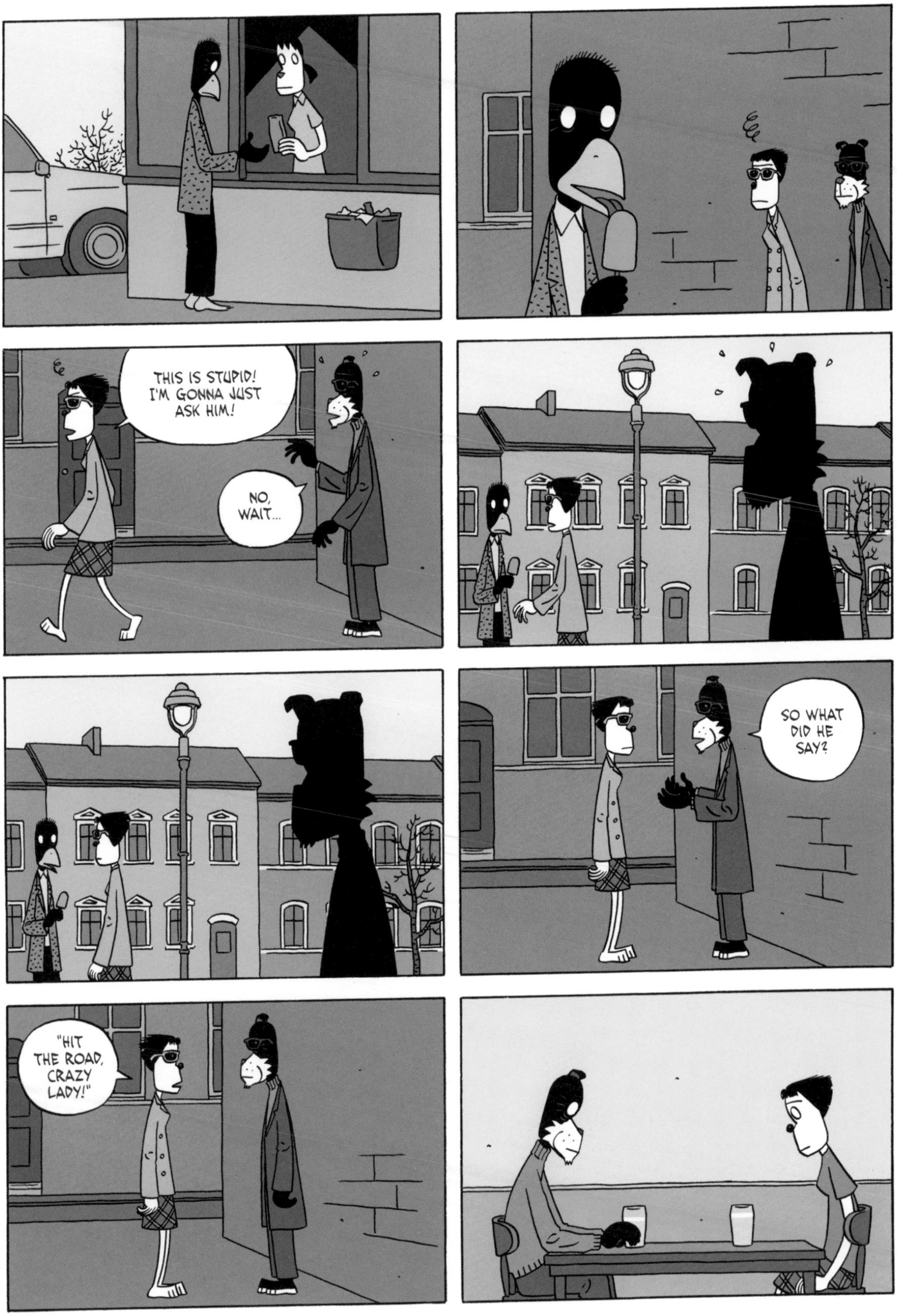
THIS IS STUPID! I'M GONNA JUST ASK HIM!
NO, WAIT...
SO WHAT DID HE SAY?
"HIT THE ROAD, CRAZY LADY!"

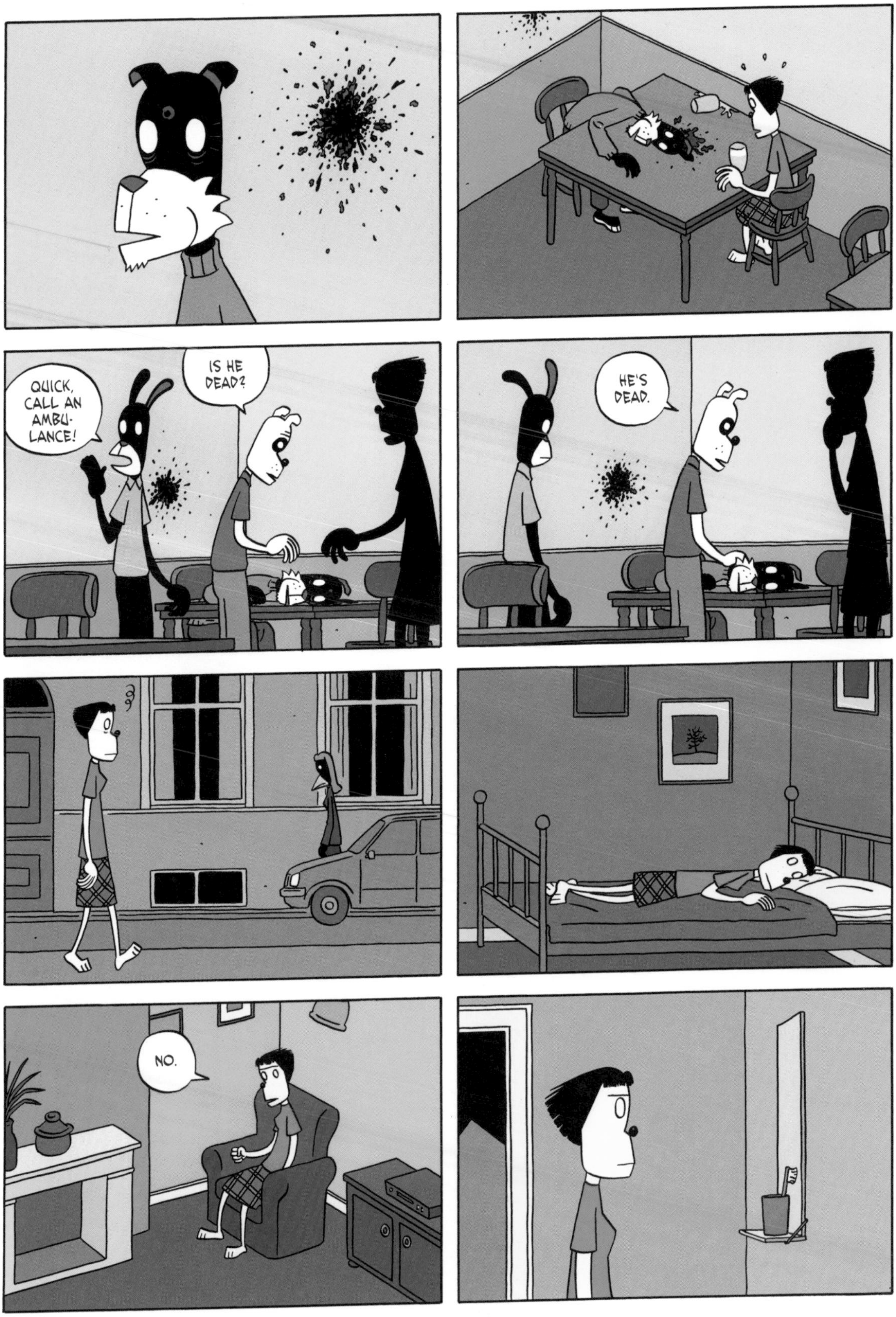
QUICK, CALL AN AMBU-LANCE!
IS HE DEAD?
HE'S DEAD.
NO.

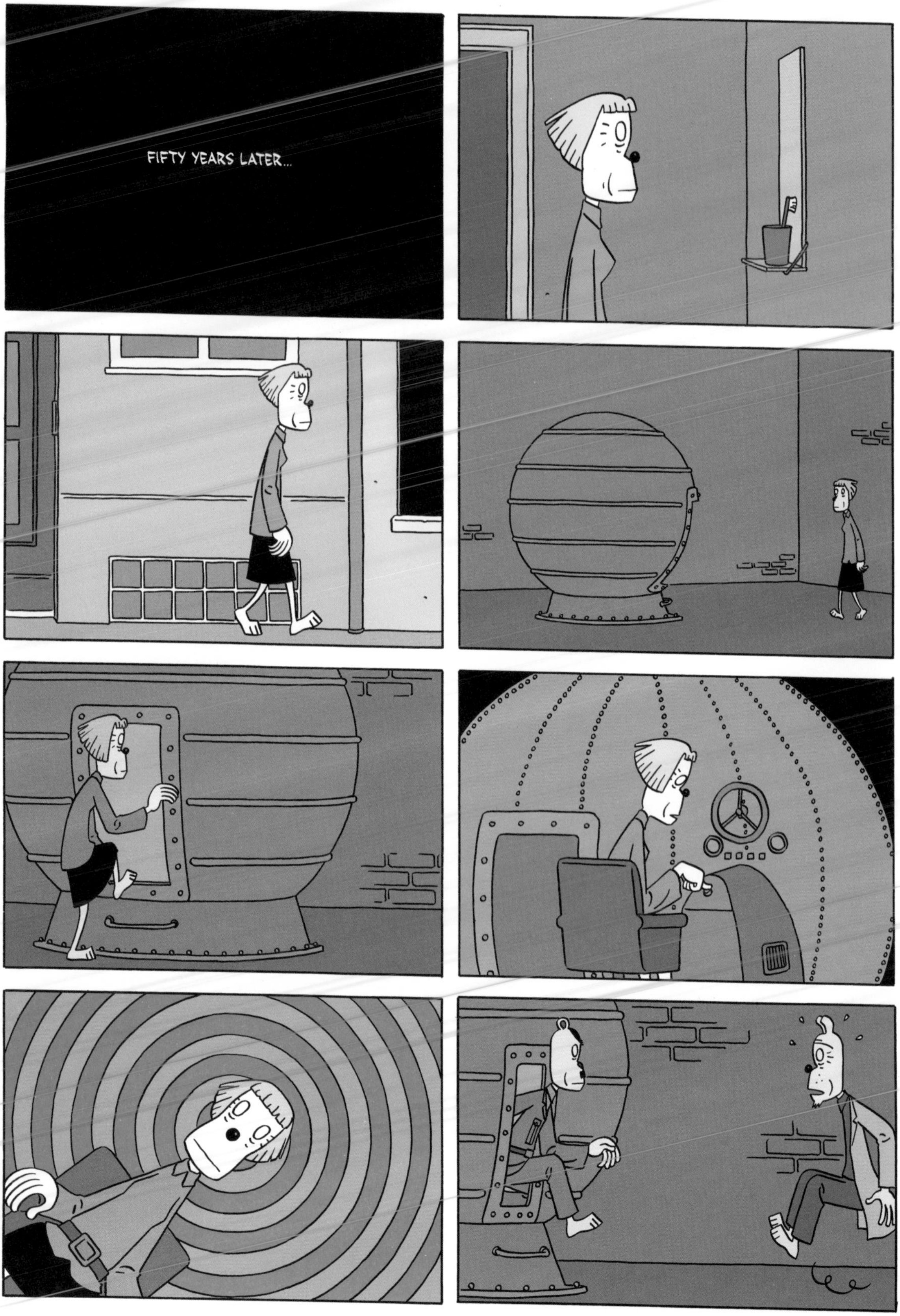
FIFTY YEARS LATER...

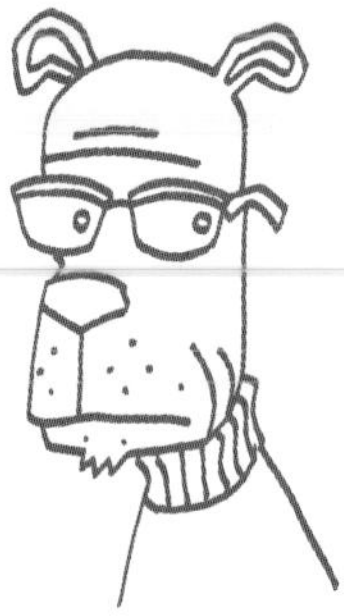

OTHER BOOKS BY JASON:

Why Are You Doing This? (2005)
The Left Bank Gang (2006)
I Killed Adolf Hitler (2007)
The Last Musketeer (2008)
Pocket Full of Rain (2008)
Low Moon (2009)
Werewolves of Montpellier (2010)
Almost Silent (2010 COMPILATION)
What I Did (2010 COMPILATION)
Isle of 100,000 Graves (2011)
Athos in America (2012)
Lost Cat (2013)
If You Steal (2015)
On the Camino (2017)

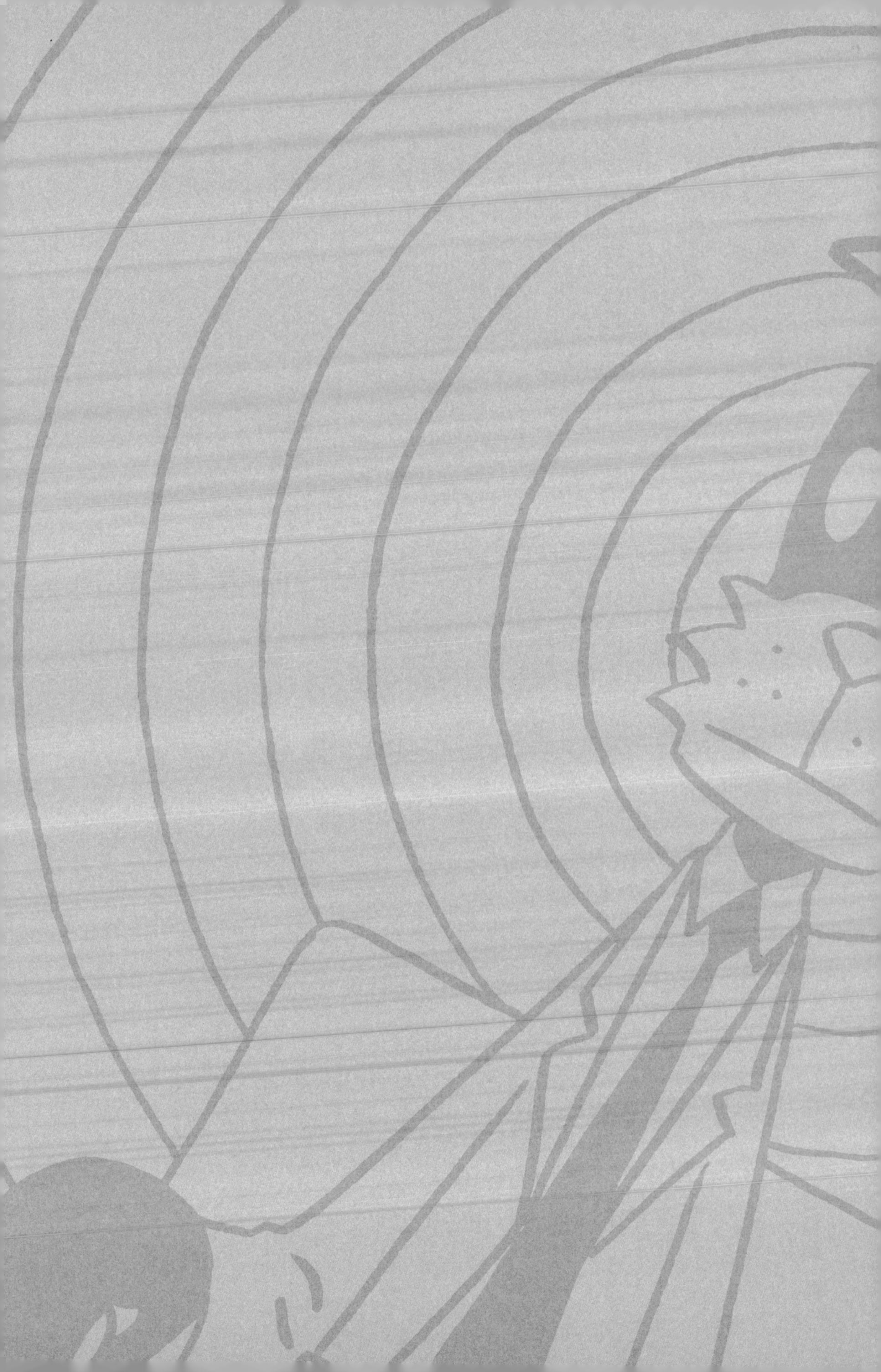